THE SCOTT HOLLAND MEMORIAL LECTURES 1969

RELIGION AND THE TRANSFORMATION OF SOCIETY

THE SCOTT HOLLAND MEMORIAL LECTURES

1 1922. R. H. Tawney, *Religion and the Rise of Capitalism*

2 1925 C. E. Osborne, *The Secular State in Relation to 'Christian Ideals'*

3 1928. William Temple (Bishop of Manchester), *Christianity and the State*

4 1930. A. D. Lindsay (Master of Balliol), *Christianity and Economics*

5 1933. Walter Moberley (Vice-Chancellor, Manchester University), *The Ethics of Punishment*

6 1936. S. C. Carpenter, *The Biblical View of Life*

7 1943. L. S. Thornton, CR, *Christ and Human Society – A Biblica. Interpretation*

8 1946. M. B. Reckitt, *Maurice to Temple – A Century of the Social Movement in the Church of England*

9 1949. V. A. Demant, *Religion and the Decline of Capitalism*

10 1952. D. M. Mackinnon, *The Humility of God*

11 1956. Joachim Wach: *Sociology of Religion.* (Professor Wach died before the lectures were delivered)

12 1960. A. R. Vidler, *Social Catholicism in France*

13 1964. A. M. Ramsey (Archbishop of Canterbury), *Sacred and Secular*

14 1966. G. B. Bentley, *The Church, Morality and the Law*

15 1969. Monica Wilson, *Religion and the Transformation of Society—A Study in Social Change in Africa*

RELIGION AND THE TRANSFORMATION OF SOCIETY

A STUDY IN SOCIAL CHANGE IN AFRICA

by

MONICA WILSON

Professor of Social Anthropology
School of African Studies
University of Cape Town

CAMBRIDGE · AT THE UNIVERSITY PRESS
1971

Published by the Syndics of the Cambridge University Press
Bentley House, 200 Euston Road, London N.W.1
American Branch: 32 East 57th Street, New York, N.Y.10022

Library of Congress Catalogue Card Number: 73–134622

ISBN: 0 521 07991 8

Printed in Great Britain by
C. Tinling & Co. Ltd London and Prescot

CONTENTS

DEDICATION

To Godfrey, Francis, and Timothy, for in conversations with them the ideas in this book have emerged

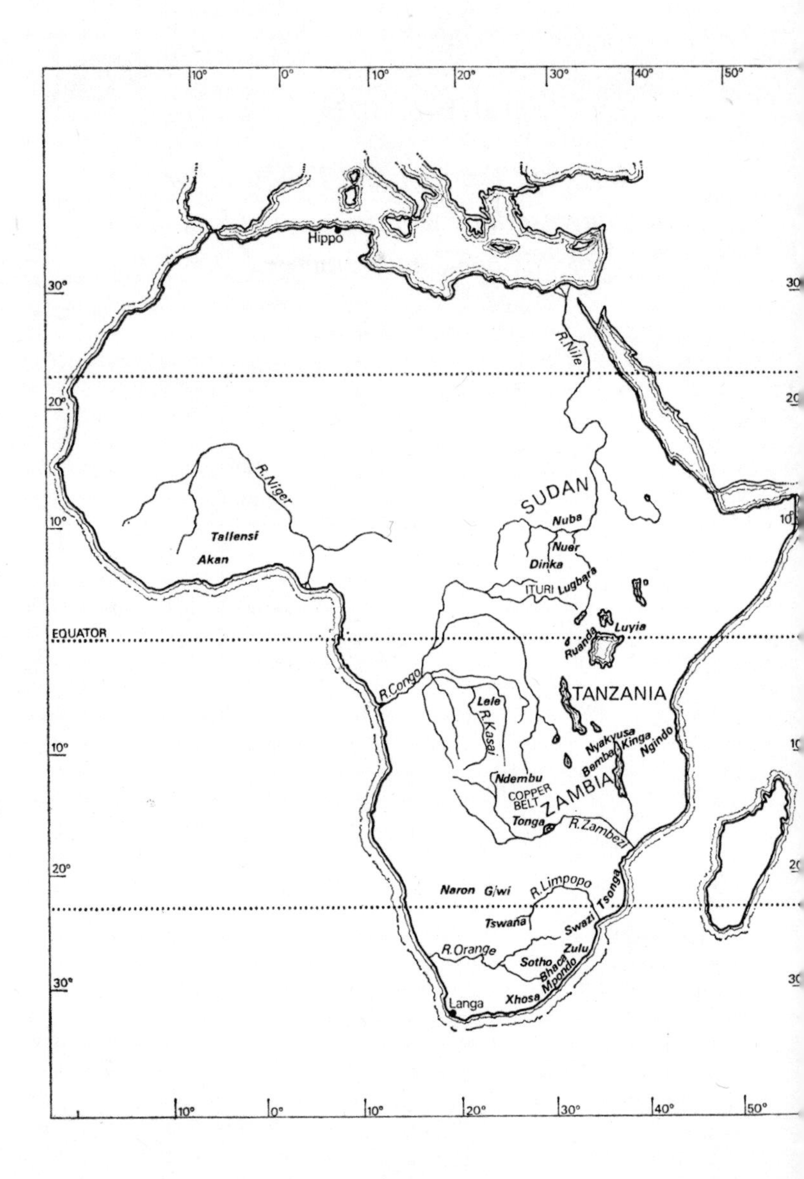

10°
0°
10°
20°
30°
40°
50°
30°
20°
10°
EQUATOR
10°
20°
30°
Hippo
R.Nile
R.Niger
Tallensi
Akan
SUDAN
Nuba
Nuer
Dinka
ITURI
Lugbara
Luyia
Ruanda
R.Congo
Lele
R.Kasai
TANZANIA
Nyakyusa
Kinga
Ngindo
Bemba
Ndembu
COPPER BELT
ZAMBIA
Tonga
R.Zambezi
Naron
G/wi
R.Limpopo
Tsonga
Tswana
Swazi
R.Orange
Zulu
Sotho
Bhaca
Mpondo
Xhosa
Langa

I. CHANGE IN SCALE

The Scott Holland Lectures began with a study of the relation between religious and economic change: *Religion and the Rise of Capitalism.* I dare follow on with reflections on the relation between religion and the radical social changes of our time, not only economic changes.

There are two characteristics of contemporary change in society: rapidity and pervasiveness. Social change has often been a 'shy sideways, crablike movement' (it is E. M. Forster's description) but in our day Cancer turns to Pegasus, and bolts, as Dr Leach has shown.[1]

I start with four assumptions. First, that there are regularities in the social field. Here anthropologists and sociologists differ from many (though not all) historians who are so preoccupied with the uniqueness of events that they doubt the existence of regularities in history. Anthropologists watching many and diverse societies cannot escape the conclusion that there are regularities. Our chief tool is *comparison*; like the zoologists from whom we sprang in Cambridge, we find it useful to compare related sorts and to inquire into the reasons for the detailed variations.

The second assumption is that if there are regularities these are discoverable.

The third, that there are conditions of social living comparable, in some degree, to biological conditions of life.

The fourth assumption is that different aspects of a society are interdependent, but that they have a relative autonomy.

Let us examine more closely the assumption that there are

[1] E. R. Leach, *A Runaway World?* The Reith Lectures, 1967 (London, 1968).

conditions of social living. Certain institutions *must* exist; that is, we have not found a society without them and until we do, the hypothesis that they are a condition of social living holds. There is always a family of some sort – parents and children – though the degree to which this elementary group is detached from a wider kinship unit, and the part taken by the father in providing for wife and child and training the children, varies. There is always a wider community of some sort also, whether it is a hunting band or a pastoral horde, or a village or town, and children may grow up almost as dependent on their age-mates as on kin. What has been peculiar to urban middle-class Europe is the degree to which parents and young children have been isolated from a wider kin group and from neighbours. A middle-class suburban house became a citadel in a way in which a room in a slum tenement or a hut in an African village was not. There is always law and custom: we need not delay to discuss the line between different sorts of obligatory behaviour, and the sanctions that enforce it, but everywhere individuals are obliged to observe certain rules within their community. There is always a system of beliefs, and judgement on right and wrong, and the celebration of rituals or ceremonials expressing beliefs and values, which together make up a people's religion or ideology.

Whether or not they believe in a transcendental God, men make assumptions about the intrinsic nature of the universe which guide their choices in everyday affairs: life after death exists or does not exist; man succeeds by his own exertions or by the grace of God; what happens to the individual is accident or design; love is stronger than hate or it is not. The notion that a man can exist without making any assumptions, and without making choices based on assumptions, is false. It is comparable to supposing that an anthropologist can make an investigation without any preconceived ideas. Language itself means that he starts with certain classifications, certain categories of thought.

From the point of view of the anthropologist all ultimate beliefs are comparable whether they assert or deny the existence of God. Humanists, Marxists, and Christians alike have ultimate beliefs and values to which everyday choices are related. From the point of view of the Christian those societies with transcendental beliefs – which assert a reality beyond what we can touch and see or measure – are distinct. In these lectures I use *religion* to mean transcendental beliefs and values, and rituals which express them; and *ideology* to mean ultimate beliefs and values which deny the existence of any transcendental reality.[1] Such beliefs and values are also expressed in symbolic action which I call *ceremonial*, distinguishing it from *ritual* which refers to some supposed transcendental reality. These are rough and ready distinctions but convenient for my purpose.

Systems of beliefs and values and the celebration of rituals are but the wrapping of personal religion – of a man's inner life – his relations with God and his neighbour; but the expression in dogma, action, and ritual are all that the outsider sees, and therefore all that the anthropologist can analyse.

The line between biological and social necessity is not sharp, for animal groups have many of the same basic needs as human groups, as will be shown later.

The fourth assumption, that different aspects of a society are interdependent but have a relative autonomy, is particularly pertinent to a study of religion. A series of African societies which have been described by anthropologists –

[1] In this terminology *apartheid* in South Africa is religion not ideology, since it is spoken of as the creation of God.

the Nuer, the Dinka, the Lugbara, the Bemba, the Ndembu, the Nyakyusa, and many others – show a clear connection between religious forms and the whole society.[1] Such a connection is generally accepted by anthropologists.[2] But there is no absolute determination of religion by technology, economy, kinship grouping, or political structure. One cannot read off the religion from the economy, or the economy from the religion, though each shapes the other. One of the problems for anthropologists is to measure this autonomy, first by comparing a series of societies with similar economies (e.g. a series of hunting peoples, or of subsistence cultivators), and analysing how their religious beliefs and practices differ, and secondly by observing how religion changes as hunters become herders, or cultivators, or herders become machine minders. The symbols change – the attributes of God, or gods, the nature of the offerings to them – the location of the altar, the worshipping group (i.e. those who pray together), and the values expressed, but some of the old dogmas may remain.

Thus a family which has been used to expressing itself in terms of a pastoral economy, finding itself unable to celebrate traditional rituals in towns, substitutes a birthday party or commemoration dinner in place of the traditional sacrifice of an animal after birth and after a funeral, but members may still pray to the shades of their ancestors. In spite of piles of mission reports and anthropological books which discuss religion, we have few detailed accounts of how religious

[1] E. E. Evans-Pritchard, *Nuer Religion* (Oxford, 1956), *passim*; G. Lienhardt, *Divinity and Experience* (Oxford, 1961), *passim*; J. Middleton, *Lugbara Religion* (London, 1960), *passim*; Monica Wilson, *Communal Rituals of the Nyakyusa* (London, 1959), pp. 216-23.

[2] C. Geertz, 'Religion as a Cultural System', in *Anthropological Approaches to the Study of Religion* (ed. M. Benton, London, 1966), pp. 1-2.

beliefs and practices have actually changed in a given community. It is only through comparative studies of this sort that we can define how far autonomy of the religious aspect has extended.

There is a curious inclination to suppose that religious, but not scientific, ideas are invalidated by being related to society. Ideas are not necessarily untrue because they have been shaped by the society in which they emerge. What is false is to suppose they can escape reformulation as societies change. Christ specifically taught that his revelation was not complete: 'I have yet many things to say unto you, but ye cannot bear them now. Howbeit when he, the Spirit of truth, is come, he will guide you into all truth.'[1] To me this implies two things: first that creeds are as tentative as scientific hypotheses. The difficulty is to recognize that the reality does not depend upon the formulation: God exists though men quarrel over his attributes. An honest Christian may struggle all his life with doubts;[2] we are past the dogmatic certainty of medieval or Victorian times and back to the position of John's disciples who, when sent to ask Jesus who he was, were told to look at the evidence for themselves. 'Tell John what things ye have seen and heard; how the blind see and the lame walk, the lepers are cleansed, the deaf hear, the dead are raised, to the poor the gospel is preached.'[3]

The second implication is that the awe-inspiring discoveries of science are part of the leading of the Spirit. They are indeed a fruit of men looking at the evidence.

[1] John 16: 12-13.

[2] Mark 9:24. Cf. L. Newbigin, *Honest Religion for Secular Man* (London, 1966), p. 98: 'The life of faith is a continually renewed victory over doubt.'

[3] Luke 7:20-2.

You will notice that anthropologists and theologians are asking different questions. The theologians ask whether a given belief is true or false. The anthropologist asks how it is related to other aspects of the society, and what effect it has on social relationships. Theologians of every society and every generation incline to think they have the final answer. Anthropologists sometimes speak as if they had also, though our studies are still in swaddling clothes. It is only seventy years since systematic fieldwork began.

In their investigations of small societies most anthropologists have used static models: that is they have pretended that the societies they were observing were not changing. Even some of the very best studies on Africa, such as that on the Nuer, have been distorted in this way. Nuer religion cannot be comprehended without taking account of the Christian kingdom of Nubia that existed on the Upper Nile until the sixteenth century,[1] for the difference between Nuer ideas of God, and those of peoples further south in Africa, is only intelligible in terms of Nuer history.

In these lectures, therefore, I try to look at societies in two dimensions; to analyse functional relations in space and in time. This is very difficult. E. M. Forster warned long ago of the danger of referring 'improperly' to time.[2] The historians concentrate on what happened – the succession of events – and the best of them demonstrate *why* things happened, analysing connections in time. The anthropologists have concentrated on *what is*, and the interaction of existing institutions. Both approaches meet in direct observation, and the first lecturer in this series, Tawney, once said: 'What historians need is not more documents but stronger boots.'[3]

[1] A. J. Arkel, *A History of the Sudan to 1821* (London, 1955), p. 197.
[2] E. M. Forster, *Aspects of the Novel* (London, 1927), p. 45.
[3] Quoted, W. K. Hancock, *Country and Calling* (London, 1954), p. 95.

We anthropologists are good on boots: we have been walking about Africa and other places for some time. So there is hope of a fruitful marriage between studies in time and in space.

Anthropologists have long pressed the advantage of using small-scale models about which the relevant facts can be encompassed in one lifetime, but to be useful the model must be one that *moves*. I shall use some of the small societies of Africa as they move from isolation to wider interaction to demonstrate the part played by religion in society, and how that part changes. I take heed of Forster, but press on all the same.

It is argued that the most general change going on in society is a change in scale, i.e. a change in the number of people interacting and the closeness of their interaction.[1] There is general agreement among anthropologists about the reality of increase in numbers of people interacting: not only are formerly isolated societies drawn into wider relations, but there is cumulative increase in population. Both processes have been most conspicuous during the past four hundred years. Changes in the nature of interaction are more debatable. Durkheim thought that the total amount of interaction increased: that people grew more and more dependent upon one another. It can be argued that the amount of interaction remains constant, but is more or less spread out, for as villagers begin to depend upon the world of strangers, they are less dependent upon each other, and on their kinsfolk in the same or other villages.[2] But whether Durkheim or his critics are right, none doubt that people interact in wider and wider circles; that this applies to more people as education and travel become more common, no longer the

[1] G. and M. Wilson, *The Analysis of Social Change* (Cambridge, 1945).
[2] *ibid.*, pp. 25-30, 39-41.

preserve of clerics, or literati; and that trade with what were once remote villages swells.

The increase in scale applies in time as well as in space. Small societies have a short time depth, all history being squeezed into ten or twelve generations. I knew people who were convinced that their ancestors had been without fire ten generations ago.[1] For them time began then. Literate societies have a longer time depth, and it is conspicuous that as they expand in space, time stretches back. The exploration of space and the exploration of the past go hand in hand, and in our generations both have been dependent upon developments in mathematics and physics. Radiocarbon dating has stretched our view of history as satellites have explored the universe. Men land on the moon and man the tool-maker is traced back one-and-a-half million years in Africa. Whether archaeologists are reporting on Africa, America, or Oceania, one phrase recurs: 'Dating has been revised. These tools are much earlier than was supposed.'

Men's view of history depends upon the society in which they live. In the small isolated societies the golden age is always in the past, and conservatism which, after all, is a condition of survival in a preliterate society, is highly valued. What is lost by one generation among preliterate people is lost for good. Change occurs, but often it is slow, and people may not admit to changing at all. Survivors from a Dutch ship, wrecked off the southern coast of Africa in 1686, spent three years among the Xhosa people, and learnt to speak the language.[2] After their rescue these men gave a detailed account of the Xhosa people to the Commander of the Cape. If that account is compared with eye-witness reports

[1] M. Wilson, *Communal Rituals*, pp. 1-16.

[2] D. Moodie, *The Record*, 1838-42 (reprint Cape Town, 1960).

of the mid-nineteenth century it can be shown that Xhosa society had changed remarkably little during nearly two hundred years. Moreover the Xhosa constantly defended their customs as being the customs of their ancestors – *amasiko*. They identified piety with conservatism.

A large-scale society is quite different. In it the Kingdom of Heaven, or a secular Utopia, lies in the future. Heaven is something towards which men strive. A messiah is awaited. Development in techniques and in scientific knowledge is valued, and spoken of as 'progress'. Many Victorians thought 'progress' applied to the moral field also, and my generation was dismayed when two wars and the horrors of concentration camps showed how hate as well as love might be nourished by growing knowledge and skill. The expectation of change is sometimes distorted into a cult of novelty, change being sought for its own sake. But without such exaggerations, the recognition that a society is fluid, that men themselves have the power to shape it, is itself a force for change, and responsibility in a revolutionary age implies acceptance of that power. Dr Leach's admonition to accept the responsibility of power was plain behind the fireworks of his Reith lectures.

It is a mistake to suppose that history has been recognized as significant only in Hebrew and Christian societies. Whether in a small community of cultivators or a great civilization like that of China, what is told as history always provides some sort of social charter. But the charter may be static: it may describe a single revolution, such as the arrival of chiefs, or of a ruling aristocracy which differed in race, and this single event is conceived as setting history for all time, because the duty of descendants is to follow exactly the pattern set by the fathers. There are numerous examples of this from Africa. Or the charter may define a cyclical view of history, in which each dynasty is thought of as making all things new, as Dr Needham has shown.[1]

The linear view of history which assumes a continuous *development* is spoken of by some theologians as peculiarly Christian. I suggest it is linked with increase in scale and that it appears in non-Christian societies also. You will remember that St Paul gained a ready hearing in Athens because Athenians of the first century A.D. already had a passion for something new,[2] and Dr Needham has shown that the expectation of development – cumulative advance – was there in nineteenth-century China.[3] But there is a measure of autonomy between men's relations in society and the ideas they conceive. The story of the Garden of Eden is a typical myth of a small society. The leap to a much wider view appears in Isaiah,[4] in an Israel which was indeed literate and trading through the Mediterranean and North Asia, and eastward to India, but was not yet wide-scale in a modern sense. Religious understanding was far ahead of the everyday pattern of social relationships.

Sir Kenneth Clark has suggested that the mark of civilization is 'a sense of permanence',[5] and he sees its expression primarily in stone buildings and in books. Permanence was thought of in Africa in terms of the lineage which continued through time, and which was symbolized by breeding stock, the succouring clump of bananas, or the cutting taken from a tree on a grave and planted in the new homestead when men moved. The trees surrounding a chief's grave formed a

[1] J. Needham, *Time and Eastern Man* (Royal Anthropological Institute, London, 1965), p. 6.

[2] Acts 17:21.

[3] Needham, p. 31.

[4] Isaiah 14:32. Cf. G. Adam Smith, *The Book of Isaiah* (London, 1896), I, 282-7.

[5] Kenneth Clark, *Civilization* (London, 1970), p. 14.

sacred grove which served as a cathedral – men worshipped there – and such groves survived through many generations. Trees and clumps of amaryllis were also used as boundary marks between chiefdoms and fields, and they, too, reflected a feeling of long-established rights in the country occupied.[1] The sense of permanence is not confined to literate peoples, though the span of time pictured extends with scale.

The drive to increase in scale is complex. The economic element is often dominant, men extending their relationships because trade with those at a distance is profitable. This has been conspicuous within the last four hundred years. But the drive to expansion of relations is also religious as men travel to distant places to preach, to spread the gospel. The simple-minded interpretation of the Christian and Muslim missionary as simply a tool of imperialism, or economic expansion, is not tenable, though it is perfectly true that missionaries aided economic expansion and were often used by imperial governments. Thirty years ago I watched changes going on in a pagan society that were directly due to Christian teaching and not economic pressures. Wealthy men, in a country in which land was still plentiful, chose to remain monogamists, because they were Christians, rather than invest their wealth in marrying several wives which, in terms of that place and time, was a profitable thing to do. A third inducement to wider interaction comes from love of adventure, or curiosity – wondering what the people beyond the next line of hills are like, and enjoying their company when you find them. All these inducements – the economic, the religious, the hedonist – are well documented in the frontier history of South Africa.[2]

[1] M. Wilson, *Communal Rituals*, pp. 54-6, 70, 73-5, 88.

[2] M. Wilson and L. Thompson (eds), *The Oxford History of South Africa* (Oxford, 1969), I, 238.

Change in scale – the range of relations and intensity of interaction in wider relations – has implications already hinted at in different views of history. I shall pick out those implications which are particularly relevant to religion. I stand by the argument set forth in *The Analysis of Social Change* twenty-five years ago, and shall summarize parts of it, but I want to expand it in certain directions.

It was argued that extension in the range of relations was directly linked to the development of tools and techniques, the growth of scientific knowledge, and increase of productivity. Each of these is connected with the others, and they are both the fruit of and lead to specialization and diversity. The mark of the large-scale society, in contrast with the small, is the extent of specialization and diversity which can be traced in the practical, intellectual, and emotional aspects of life. Now this growth of specialization is conspicuous within the religious aspect. In the very small societies priests are not distinguished from senior kinsmen and chiefs, nor magicians from scientists, and no general distinction is made between sacred and secular. One field-worker after another reports that though analysis may require such a distinction it is not given in the facts they describe, or apparent in the vernacular they have used. Durkheim, who assumed that the distinction was universal, was no field-worker.

The structural aspect of specialization is a variety of associations embodying special interests, and as societies diversify these increase very fast. One of the associations embodying a special interest is the Church, *as an organization*. We can distinguish between the Church as the community of the faithful called by God, and the organization – the association, the anthropologist would say – which men join. In medieval Europe the association was coterminous with the community: it has never been so in Africa or Asia and it has ceased to be so in Europe, therefore its character as an organization created by those sharing a common interest becomes clearer. The splintering of the Catholic Church was in part a diversification, a rejection of uniformity.

The secularization about which there is so much talk is partly this process of specialization. In contemporary society sacred and secular, priests and laymen, religious and other organizations are distinguished. We know when we stop to think about it that for the Christian there are no non-religious activities: God pervades life. But it is also true that there are activities, such as worship, of which the explicit purpose is religious, and organizations and persons dedicated to religious ends. Many people argue that specialization has gone too far in the intellectual aspect (in universities for example) as well as in the religious. But specialization, as Adam Smith showed,[1] has been the condition of that enormous development in techniques, scientific knowledge, and productivity which distinguishes the large from the small-scale society.

Secularization in the modern world is in part specialization, but it is something more. It contains an implication that the sacred is irrelevant. Not only are priests and scientists distinguished but the scientist is held to be important, the priest unimportant.

A number of anthropologists from Frazer onward, and many other people, have thought that science would replace religion; that as technical control increased religion would be edged out altogether. Evidence can be cited to show that dependence upon magic, and sacrifice, and on prayer diminishes fastest in just those fields in which technical control is

[1] Adam Smith, *The Wealth of Nations* (1776; 1904 edition, London), I, 5-18.

greatest. Do men pray for rain when they can irrigate the land? Do they pray to avert typhus when they can inoculate against it and exterminate lice? Is God relevant in the large society? It is easy to show that man's control over himself is very limited: he can make the desert blossom as the rose but he has not stopped fighting over it, and any moment he might create something far worse in a radio-active waste. He may obliterate typhus but the kind of competitive society he has created fosters loneliness and perhaps mental disorders. I don't think men have become as gods, as Dr Leach argued: rather they are small boys with sharp tools. We are still remarkably inept at arranging relationships between men. Indeed, technical development makes international relations more dangerous, as nation after nation is armed with atomic and biological weapons but we fail to achieve agreement on control of their use. The international picture is horribly like that of the hunting bands of southern Africa who were armed with poisoned arrows so dangerous that a scratch could kill a man, and the loss of one or two hunters endangered the survival of the whole band. Impotence in managing social relations may grow as well as diminish in terms of the tools we command, and that impotence drives us back to prayer.

But the real answer to Frazer and his followers who think that science will replace religion is that science does not make choices. Religion does. And choice extends with scale.

Very small societies are homogeneous and the members share the same beliefs though they may sacrifice to different ancestors. Large societies are diverse and the sort of pressures to conformity that exist in an isolated preliterate community are matched in the modern world only in certain sub-groups such as boys' preparatory schools, small religious sects, and some firms and professions. Our society as a whole admits of a wide diversity in beliefs and values, and a choice of sub-groups exists.

Diversity in a society implies a relative autonomy of thought and action: without it no specialist can exercise his specialism. If the artist's creation or the scientist's hypotheses are censored by his society, and he cannot communicate them to his fellows – something that is happening in my own country – then his work as a specialist is hampered. A form of autonomy which we particularly cherish is freedom of conscience: freedom to worship as we choose. But freedom and diversity are always within some accepted framework. Argument turns on what framework – what general rules – are acceptable. For example, colonial governments, and their heirs, the independent states in Africa, have enforced a conception of 'natural justice'[1] which precludes the execution of supposed witches, though many village people still think of those they accuse of witchcraft as murderers. And my own country, South Africa, calls itself Christian and boasts religious freedom, but there are pressures towards confining worship within the framework of racial separation.

The practical problem, particularly acute in new states, is how to combine political unity and freedom, common values and toleration. The spectre of fragmentation now stalks Africa and India, and the fear of it has been at the root of much cruelty in the Soviet Union.

Diversity and change are closely linked, since social change consists first in the appearance of a difference in society, and then in an increase in the number of people acting differently from their neighbours (e.g. the establishment of a mission school where no school has existed, an

[1] Traditional law was recognized except where 'repugnant to natural justice'.

increase in the number of children attending, and then an increase in the number and variety of schools).

As societies increase in scale, impersonal relations become more important. Face-to-face relationships form a small proportion of the network of relationships on which a man depends and not even all the face-to-face relations are really personal. We take it for granted that trade, government, law, which are very personal in a small society, should be impersonal in a large society; and we think it right that it should be so. I remember a Nyakyusa chief, in what was then Tanganyika, explaining in 1935, that he found it much more difficult to judge cases than formerly, because strangers had begun to come to his court. He did not know them or their families, therefore, he said, he could not tell whether their evidence was true or false. Formerly he had known everyone who came, and the character of their kinsmen, and had judged accordingly. But we choose jurymen who have *no* personal ties with the accused, holding that personal ties preclude impartiality.

Impersonal relations are inevitable in the large society – no individual can know everyone upon whom he depends – he does not have time. And in some degree he can choose whom he will know personally. Harvey Cox has argued that impersonal relations contribute to the city man's freedom:[1] because such relationships are taken for granted in the city, a man may choose those persons with whom to establish personal ties, whereas a villager is required to accept personal ties with all other villagers whether they are compatible or not.

It may be argued that the development of impersonal relationships contributes equally to a man's intellectual

[1] Harvey Cox, *The Secular City* (paperback edition, London, 1966), pp. 41-9.

development. They are a condition of growth of a conception of impersonal causation. Isolated people interpret events in personal terms: less isolated people in less personal terms. Isolation applies (as I have said) in time and space, and the preliterate, or illiterate, are more isolated than the literate. Men who interpret events in purely personal terms seek a personal cause of misfortune. To them illness and death are sent by an enemy, and the important thing is to discover the identity of that enemy. Almost forty years ago in Pondoland, when typhus was killing men, an Mpondo teacher discussing the cause of his brother's death remarked: 'I accept this typhus is spread by lice, but why did the infected louse bite my brother, not me? Who sent the louse?'[1]

The growth of science has implied a concentration on proximate causes and a suspension of argument regarding ultimate causes, though the question of ultimate cause still nags even in a society dominated by scientific thinking, like ours. Men keeping asking: 'Why did it have to happen to me?' 'Why was my child run over?' And they are not comforted by talk of accident proneness or statistical probability.

The notion of impersonal causation implies some measure of detachment from self. Such detachment is both a condition of and a fruit of scientific analysis – that is the study of impersonal causation.[2] It is something that we value greatly. But alone it is unsatisfying, for we are, after all *persons*, and personality does not diminish with increase in scale.

Now how does increase in impersonal relationships and impersonal thinking, which can be observed directly, fit with the idea that evolution is the trend towards the personal? A former Chancellor of Cambridge University, Jan Christian Smuts, set forth the argument that evolution implied a pro-

[1] Monica Hunter, *Reaction to Conquest* (London, 1936), p. 274.
[2] G. and M. Wilson, pp. 89-90.

gressive development of the personal.[1] The theme has been pursued in the writings of Teilhard de Chardin who speaks of evolution as 'an ascent towards consciousness'.[2] Perhaps it might be better translated as a growth of self-awareness.

Self-awareness is not something that begins suddenly in man. Personal relations begin among animals as Lorentz and other ethologists have shown. He finds no personal relations among insects, a horde of rats, or shoal of fish, but he finds them among geese,[3] and they are clearly there among apes. I had the good fortune to spend days watching a baboon pack at Cape Point with the late Ronald Hall, and no one who did so, and learnt to distinguish the animals within the pack, could doubt some degree of self-awareness among them. There are even indications that incest taboos have begun in baboon packs, sure evidence of the awareness of individual ties through time.

Personal relations are always present in human communities. In very small-scale societies, such as those of hunters, there is virtually no impersonal relationship, and the distinction between men and animals, or man and the rest of the universe, is less sharp than it is with us. Dream and waking experience are identified in a fashion that is more than just a matter of speech. As a field-worker in Africa when discussing some kinds of personal experience, I found it necessary to ask: 'Were you awake or asleep when this happened?'

There is a growth in self-awareness as men move from isolated preliterate societies to large, literate societies. The most important factor in this growth is ability to communi-

[1] J. C. Smuts, *Holism and Evolution* (London, 1926), pp. 261-89.

[2] Teilhard de Chardin, *The Phenomenon of Man* (London, 1959), p. 258.

[3] K. Lorentz, *On Aggression* (London, 1966), pp. 123-7.

cate, and all human communities have language. This is their distinguishing characteristic: that which differentiates them from any baboon pack or chimpanzee band. They all have music and dancing, and forms of symbolic action which I shall later define as ritual or ceremonial. The pygmies of the Congo forest drum and sing in praise of the forest on which they depend, and express their relations with other pygmies in the ritual of the *molimo*, the sacred trumpet.[1] Naron or G/wi of the Kalahari dance their view of God and man in the moonlight miming the eland, gemsbok, or ostrich which were to them the symbols of plenty and well-being,[2] and all of them are hunting peoples living in isolated bands – the smallest-scale societies we know. Most peoples have painting and carving, and some have writing and mathematics. Self-awareness increases as a child learns to manipulate his mother tongue, and the symbolic actions understood in his group, but I think this growth is limited by the techniques available to him. I think it advances further as people learn to read and to reflect on abstract ideas. There has surely been an increase in self-awareness in Western Europe since the work of Freud became familiar: a difference in outlook due to the development of psychiatry has been conspicuous between my own generation and that which preceded it. His Grace the Archbishop of Canterbury spoke of psychiatry enlarging the areas of conscious moral decision in his Scott Holland lectures five years ago.[3]

Growing self-awareness is apparent in the rapidly changing states of Africa. Dr Kenneth Kaunda, President of Zambia, writes: 'The question being asked all over Black Africa is

[1] C. M. Turnbull, *The Forest People* (London, 1961), pp. 132-49.

[2] D. Bleek, *The Naron* (Cambridge, 1928), pp. 22-7; G. B. Silberbauer, *Bushman Survey* (Gaberones, 1965), pp. 97-9.

[3] A. M. Ramsey, *Sacred and Secular* (London, 1965), p. 69.

"Who am I?".'[1] Now Dr Kaunda has spanned in his own lifetime a period of very rapid increase in scale: his father was a village schoolmaster, and later a minister, in a remote and isolated corner of Zambia. His ties with the outside world were meagre; but Dr Kaunda himself has travelled and made friends throughout the world. Such extension of contacts drives men to a greater consciousness of their own identity.

A hundred years ago, a Cambridge lawyer, Sir Henry Maine, drew attention to the manner in which personality was increasingly recognized in law. He spoke of a movement 'from status to contract'.[2] 'Starting, as from one terminus of history, from a condition of society in which all the relations of Persons are summed up in the relations of Family, we seem to have steadily moved towards a phase of social order in which all these relations arise from the free agreement of Individuals. In Western Europe the progress achieved in this direction has been considerable. Thus the status of the Slave has disappeared – it has been superseded by the contractual relation of the servant to his master. The status of the Female under Tutelage, if the tutelage be understood of persons other than her husband, has also ceased to exist; from her coming of age to her marriage all the relations she may form are relations of contract. So too the status of Son under Power has no true place in the law of modern European societies . . . the movement of progressive societies has hitherto been a movement from Status to Contract.' His seminal ideas grew from studies in early Roman law, and in village India; he was as eager as any anthropologist to compare different societies, and drew conclusions from the differences.

[1] K. Kaunda, *A Humanist in Africa* (London, 1966), p. 57.
[2] Henry Maine, *Ancient Law* (London, 1876), 6th ed., pp. 169-70.

This legal development continues in the Declaration of Human Rights, and in the insistence of the International Commission of Jurists that *privacy* of person should be safeguarded.

In religious terms the development is clear. In small pagan societies, such as existed in Africa, rituals were primarily directed towards the well-being of the group; towards health and fertility for the community; and the emphasis was on the fact that kinsfolk and neighbours were members one of another. *One* member of a lineage drank the poison ordeal on behalf of the lineage, and could clear or condemn it, just as all the members of a lineage shared responsibility if one were a thief. It is true that certain sacrifices were made on behalf of particular individuals, but as often as not the *cause* of their misfortune was judged to be the wrong-doing of another kinsman – a parent, or sibling, or distant ancestor. (I draw my evidence here from the Nyakyusa people of Tanzania.)

In the New Testament the worth of every individual is repeatedly asserted, and the history of the Christian Church has in part been a history of how individual worth was cherished. At the Reformation the stress was on each man judging for himself, on the freedom of individual conscience, and on individual responsibility.

Nowadays we sometimes ask whether individualism has not run amok. Lorentz tells us that the personal bond erupted with aggression; it 'is only found in animals with highly developed intra-specific aggression'.[1] And we ask ourselves whether we have paid too much for the growth of personality. I think *competition* has run amok, and that we shall discuss later, but no one who has himself lived primitive, when the individual is constantly subordinated to the group,

[1] Lorentz, pp. 126-7, 186.

can doubt the value of a growth in freedom of individual thought and expression. In a small-scale society eccentrics are not tolerated. They are likely to be accused of witchcraft or sorcery. The range of diversity permitted is very much smaller than in a modern city.

Men grow in awareness not only of themselves but of the groups in which they live. As societies increase in size their members reflect on their constitution, hence, economics, law, politics, sociology, and anthropology. The contrast with small societies whose members have great difficulty in conceptualizing the group, and analysing relationships in it, is apparent to any field-worker investigating a pre-literate and isolated people. Men in a very isolated society scarcely reflect on their institutions. But the study of society is a condition of existence for a modern man. If relationships are not understood, in some measure, the large society cannot operate. Economics, politics, sociology, anthropology are not luxuries today, but a condition of effective organization. This is more often noticed in war time than in peace.

The growth of knowledge and skill which is the mark of the large society implies more choice. The further we control our material environment the more we can choose how to use our wealth; the further medical science develops the less we are bound by biological necessities. The choices in this field frighten us; who is to decide whether a pregnancy likely to result in a deformed child is to be terminated or not? Is it only a matter for parents? Who is to decide whether or not to treat with powerful and unpleasant drugs a mongol child suffering from leukaemia? And if he is not to be treated, should a mongol with a severe chest infection be saved? Whose decision is this? Who is to decide which of several patients should be given the compatible heart available for transplantation or, more commonly, the single place available in the artificial kidney unit?

And the diverse society provides a choice of job, of recreation, of friends, of beliefs and values which is not there in the isolated homogeneous band. So with growing awareness there is growing freedom of thought and action. This is both exhilarating and frightening. Many people keep trying to evade the choices, and pretend they don't exist; or push them on to the specialist in the vain hope that they can be decided by scientific criteria. They are harking back to the isolated group where material and biological necessities press so hard, and yet further to the animal pack where most behaviour (but not all) is instinctive. Freedom of choice and self-awareness are two aspects of the same thing. Men come to know themselves as consciously they choose.

I arrive then at this paradox, that as societies increase in scale, impersonal relationships grow more important: they must do so, for, to extend Whitehead's argument, no one man can know everyone at once any more than he can know everything at once.[1] But at the same time those personal relationships that exist may grow deeper. As science and arts develop, man's potential self-awareness increases, and as he learns to know himself, his relationships with others may flower. Choice extends and love and friendship flourish best when choice is free.

Now choice is something that goes beyond science – an exact knowledge of the facts – for it implies a judgement of value; of preferring one thing to another. Many people have looked to science to make choices for them. This it can

[1] A. N. Whitehead, *Science in the Modern World* (Pelican edition, 1938) p. 184: 'No one man, no limited society of men and no one epoch can think of everything at once.'

never do, however many facts are assembled.[1] Ultimately, most parents must choose whether to have few children or many, and a community must decide whether the parents alone should choose or whether their choice be limited. Medical practitioners are entitled to some guidance as to the relative value of different lives and different qualities of life.

In this book I am trying, as an anthropologist, to analyse the implication of change in scale. I have spent my life trying to do so objectively. But also I am making a choice, a judgement of value as a Christian. Change in scale is not something a Christian can be neutral about. We are commanded to treat the stranger as a neighbour, to preach the gospel to all the world. The nature of the choice is particularly clear in my own country, where there is constant pressure to limit interaction between different racial groups. As a Christian I totally reject such limitation. The Reverend Beyers Naudé, the leader of the Christian opposition to apartheid from within, in South Africa, wrote two years ago: 'Christian missionary activity, from the journeys of St. Paul onward, may be seen as an outreaching, an encounter with the stranger, a seeking of the isolated.'[2]

As an anthropologist I attempt to analyse Christianity as one religion among others. At the same time, as a believer, I accept the gospels as a revelation of truth. The traditional religions of Africa reveal fragments of truth – much more than many missionaries have supposed. The gospels provide a fuller revelation but our formulations are far from complete. We have yet to be led by the Spirit of Truth into all truth, and seeking to understand the part of religion in society is a leading of the Spirit of Truth.

Those are the premises from which I start, and in this book

[1] John Macmurray, *The Boundaries of Science* (London, 1939).
[2] The Rev. Beyers Naudé, *Pro Veritate* (1968).

I shall both analyse relationships and make judgements of value. Fact can never be wholly separated from value as the economists Gunnar Myrdal, Kenneth Boulding, and others have shown us,[1] but I shall try to relate the value judgements to the premises which have been stated.

I have argued that the most general characteristic of the rapid change going on in society is change in scale – in the number of people interacting closely. It applies in space and time and it involves increasing specialization and diversity which are manifest in religion. Secularization is partly specialization, but for some people it has also implied that religion will be replaced by science. This is not possible, since science does not make choices, and choice does not disappear but increases with increase in scale. Impersonal relationships become more important as the number of people interacting increases, but at the same time there is a growth of self-awareness in both individuals and groups.

The next three chapters are concerned with the evidence of change in the religion of some small societies of Africa, as they expanded in scale, during this century. The concluding chapters are on the implications of change in scale for religion in contemporary society.

[1] G. Myrdal, *An American Dilemma* (New York, 1944), Appendices 1 and 2; K. E. Boulding, 'Economics as a Moral Science', *American Economic Review*, **60**, 1 (1969), 1-12.

II. THE SHADES, MEDICINES, WITCHCRAFT, AND GOD

This chapter is concerned with how the traditional religions of certain isolated societies of southern and eastern Africa have changed as these societies increased in scale. Evidence is drawn from the Nyakyusa of Tanzania, and the Nguni (Mpondo, Xhosa, Zulu, and Swazi peoples) of South Africa with whom I am familiar, and comparative evidence is cited from the Bemba, Ndembu, and Tonga of Zambia.

Among all the peoples mentioned there were four elements in the traditional religion: the cult of the shades, the belief in God, the manipulation of medicines, and the fear of witchcraft. Nyakyusa Christians used to sing a song defining the people they knew in terms of their gods. The refrain was: *Bikwiputa Kugu – To Whom do They Pray.*[1] In the song the chiefs (Nyakyusa chiefs) prayed to the *shades*, in contrast to Europeans who prayed to *money*, and Muslims who prayed to *Mohammed*. The song conveyed what these villagers noticed: that Europeans were driven by the desire for wealth; that Muslims spoke of Mohammed rather than Allah; that their pagan kin and neighbours were preoccupied with offerings to the shades. It was the cult of the shades, the ancestors, or senior dead members of the lineage, that was the principal element in pagan religion, not only among the

[1] Monica Wilson, *Rituals of Kinship among the Nyakyusa* (London, 1957), (text following title page); cf. T. S. Eliot, *The Idea of a Christian Society* (London, 1939), p. 64: 'Was our society, which had always been so assured of its superiority and rectitude, so confident of its unexamined premisses, assembled round anything more permanent than a congeries of banks, insurance companies and industries, had it any beliefs more essential than a belief in compound interest and the maintenance of dividends?'

Nyakyusa, but generally in southern and eastern Africa.

Among the Nyakyusa, ordinary people – commoners – were concerned only with immediately dead ancestors in a lineage of two or three generations but chiefs and hereditary priests made offerings to heroes or founding ancestors on behalf of chiefdoms and groups of chiefdoms. The mystical power of a dead chief was thought to extend over the country he had once ruled.

The cult of the shades was celebrated through sacrifice, prayer, and confession. The sacrifice was a feast in which dead and living kinsmen participated. The dead were repeatedly spoken of as being hungry (*bafuna ukudla ngaye*),[1] and wanting attention,[2] and sacrifice satisfied[3] them. The form of the offering varied with the economy. Cattle people like the Nguni made regular sacrifices of oxen or cows, and the altar was the cattle byre; a banana people like the Nyakyusa made their offering in the banana grove. The staple food of the Nyakyusa varied with the altitude at which they lived, and their offering varied accordingly. Only the chiefs who (according to tradition) had brought cattle to the country regularly offered cattle. A hunting people like the Ndembu made offerings at trees associated with the chase, and they might offer game as well as millet flour. Who acted as priest, and who was invoked, depended upon the form of kinship: Nyakyusa and Nguni offered principally to ancestors in the male line, Tonga and Ndembu to ancestors in the female line.

The form of offering among the Mpondo was similar to the slaughter of an animal for an honoured guest. Precisely that cut (*intsonyama*) given to the guest was eaten by the

[1] Hunter, pp. 232, 245.
[2] E. Colson, *The Plateau Tonga* (Manchester, 1962), p. 7.
[3] M. Wilson, *Communal Rituals*, p. 162.

person on whose behalf the offering was made. This was usually a sick person or a novice undergoing initiation. Honoured guest and patient or novice all wore the gall-bladder. For a guest the eating of the *intsonyama* and the wearing of the gall-bladder were a matter of prestige – he was, as it were, garlanded; but a patient or novice was required to follow the traditional form if the sacrifice was to be efficacious.

As the animal was slaughtered, the senior kinsman or kinswoman present invoked the shades, calling upon them by name. This prayer took the form of a conversation with the dead; an *expostulation* at their continued anger, a complaint at the behaviour of living kin, a praising of both living and dead;[1] for the distinction between living and dead was not at all sharp. All were members of the lineage, and they were praised by being identified with that lineage. Living and dead alike were thought to have power over their juniors. Men feared the anger of a living father as they feared the dead; sterility might be attributed to the anger of an offended aunt who was alive, or of one long dead. In Xhosa the same word (*itongo*) is actually applied to a shade and a senior living relative whose power is feared.[2]

Anger was feared, the anger of the living and the dead, of kinsmen and neighbours, and above all, anger that was unadmitted and festering in a man's heart. The only cure was for the angry man to 'speak out', to confess, to admit his anger and express good will. This idea occurs right down Africa from the Sudan to the Cape, and the same symbols of confession recur also. The commonest is blowing out water, which the Nyakyusa interpret thus: 'If a father is angry with his son or daughter he may say some day: "I

[1] Hunter, pp. 234-64.
[2] *Ibid.* pp. 231-3.

forgive you now" and spit on the ground: all the anger that is in him comes out like spit.'[1]

An ordinary Nyakyusa or Mpondo man had a very lively sense of the presence of the dead – his family shades. Once when I asked an Mpondo where the shades dwelt he waved his hand round the courtyard and cattle byre of his homestead: 'They are here, all around', and likewise a Nyakyusa spoke of little puffs of wind stirring dust and dry banana leaves in the groves around his house as evidence of the presence of his shades.

The attitude towards the shades was, however, ambivalent. Men both sought protection from the shades and feared them: men interpreted certain dreams as revelations, but were treated, in the Nyakyusa death ritual, to stop them dreaming of the dead.

The mystical element is most developed among those who practise as diviners, or clairvoyants. Their capacity to see what is hidden from ordinary men is held to be dependent upon their shades: that which is hidden is constantly revealed to them in dreams, sometimes in trances. The Nguni diviner or clairvoyant held converse with the shades in a seance during which she worked herself into an ecstasy through dancing and with the aid of a chorus clapping for her in compelling rhythm. Fasting, purging, solitude were also used as means of inducing revelation. The Nyakyusa believed that their prophets were able to foresee the future, and there were many stories about prophesies of war, of drought, and the coming of the whites.[2] As with the Nguni

[1] M. Wilson, *Rituals of Kinship*, pp. 66, 181-2, 135, 211; *Communal Rituals*, pp. 106, 139, 160-1, 217-18; cf. E. E. Evans-Pritchard, *Witchcraft, Oracles and Magic among the Azande* (Oxford, 1937), pp. 95-6; H. A. Junod, *The Life of a South African Tribe* (London, 1927), 2nd ed., 2 vols, I, 111; II, 391, 399-401, 405.

[2] M. Wilson, *Communal Rituals*, pp. 16, 29, 71-2, 164.

diviner, the source of revelation was thought to be in communion with the shades. Such beliefs are still lively. A well-known diviner, Khotsho, living in Pondoland, is commonly consulted about prospects in horse races, and sometimes he is astonishingly accurate in his predictions. In 1969, for example, he correctly predicted the winner and the horse taking second place in the Durban July Handicap, his predictions being published before the race. He attributed his foresight to the favour of his shades. But in both Nyakyusa and Nguni rituals the dead were driven off as well as sought; they brought madness as well as power.[1]

The main occasions of ritual in all these small societies were at the crises in the life of the individual – birth, initiation, marriage, and death – when both an individual and those closest to him changed their social status. At the birth ritual a child was accepted as a member of the lineage, and the mother, especially at the birth of her first child, went up in the world. At a male initiation not only the novice changed his position from boy to man, but his parents, if he were their eldest son, moved to a more senior position in society as parents of an adult man. And similarly, when a girl was initiated she changed from child to bride, or potential bride, and her mother changed in status also. The other occasions of family ritual were in sickness and misfortune, reconciliation after quarrelling, and, more rarely, thanksgiving after escape from danger.[2] The Mpondo used to give thanks when a son returned safely from a term of working on the gold mines.

[1] M. Wilson, *Rituals of Kinship*, pp. 46-54, 67-85, 122, 124, 127, 208, 215, 232.

[2] M. Wilson, *Rituals of Kinship*, pp. 186-9; Hunter, pp. 251-3; Junod, I, 71-112, 133-67, 172-82, 370-94, 464; A. I. Richards, *Land, Labour and Diet in Northern Rhodesia* (London, 1939), pp. 151-380; *Chisungu* (London, 1956), *passim*.

In the Nyakyusa cycles those who had celebrated a ritual as principals – chief mourners for parents, spouse, parents of twins, etc. – did not celebrate that ritual again. They had finished, and were apart as those who had endured. Among the Ndembu there was a further development. Most rituals were celebrated by adepts: those who had previously been through a ritual assisted a novice. The affliction came from a shade of the novice but the celebrants were not a group of kinsmen: they were those who had been afflicted in that way themselves. This was also the pattern for one Nguni ritual, the *ukuthwasa* or initiation of diviners. Thus rituals began to break out of the kinship shell, and those with a particular experience formed a worshipping group.

Rituals were celebrated on behalf of the whole community at seed time and at harvest; at the break of the rains or the summer solstice; in times of public misfortune: drought, pestilence, or war; and at the installation of a new ruler or rulers.[1]

In both public and private rituals men were preoccupied with fertility. The chiefs and their ancestors, or certain hereditary priests, were thought to control the fertility of the country: of fields, of herds, and of the community as a whole; and senior kinsmen were thought to control fertility within a lineage. As a Nyakyusa priest put it: 'the shade and the semen are brothers', and in one Nguni dialect, Bhaca, the same word (*idlozi*) is applied to shade and semen.[2]

[1] M. Wilson, *Communal Rituals, passim;* H. Kuper, *An African Aristocracy* (London, 1947), pp. 197-225; A. I. Richards, 'Social Mechanisms for the Transfer of Political Rights in Some African Tribes', *Journal of the Royal Anthropological Institute*, **90,** 2 (1960), 175-90; 'Keeping the King Divine', *Proceedings of the Royal Anthropological Institute* for 1968 (London, 1969), 23-35.

[2] *Idlozi* – semen virile in Xhosa (A. Kropf, *A Kaffir–English Dictionary* (Lovedale, 1899); *Idlozi* – departed spirit (C. M. Doke and B. W. Vilakazi, *Zulu–English Dictionary* (Johannesburg, 1964).

Health was as important as fertility, and most rituals directed towards the shades were celebrated with the express purpose of maintaining health in body and mind. Specific rituals were celebrated also for the recovery of the sick.

The shades were thought to be concerned with the observance of tradition, more especially with the precise details of ritual as handed down. Ritual custom (*lisiko*, plural *amasiko* in Xhosa) was sacred, the observance of it thought to be efficacious. Thus piety and conservatism were identified, and the individual was not free to change. I think, though it is difficult to prove this, that the stress on tradition is greatest when a remnant is standing against the tide of change, struggling to maintain what to them are the sacred customs of the ancestors. The pagan Xhosa, still standing in opposition to the 'school people' who began to accept change more than a hundred years ago, are an example. They continually speak of *amasiko* (ritual customs), whose breach is an offence to the shades. They speak of them much more than the Nyakyusa did when their traditional ritual was still generally observed. I first knew the Nyakyusa when about eighty per cent of the population celebrated most traditional rituals.

The second element in traditional religion was the idea of God. Among those peoples with whom we are particularly concerned, the Nyakyusa and Nguni, belief in a high god was shadowy. Names for Creator, the First One, existed in Zulu and Xhosa when missionaries encountered them, and some notion of God was linked with the sky, especially with the clouds, rain, thunder, and lightning. During a storm men were quiet, believing they were in the presence of divinity,[1] and twins – the evidence of fearful fecundity – were associ-

[1] Hunter, p. 302; cf. Lienhardt, pp. 29-37, 91-3.

ated with thunder and lightning.[1] But no rituals were celebrated for God, and he was not consistently distinguished from a first ancestor who dwelt beneath.[2] The shades were of the earth, the earth in which corpses were buried: they were 'those beneath' (*abapasi* in KiNyakyusa)[3] and the founding heroes were beneath also. There was no hint of the sacrificial animal taking upon it the suffering and guilt of men.

John Taylor argues that in Bantu-speaking Africa the significant fact is the contradiction of views: God is both there and not there; a sense of pervading presence is expressed but God has withdrawn.[4]

There can be no question that the idea of God was traditionally much further developed among the Nuer and Dinka of the Sudan than it was further south, that among them divinity was conceived as one, though it had many manifestations, and that the idea of atonement in sacrifice was explicit. Among them sacrifice to God was made, and 'suffering and guilt' were 'placed on the back of the sacrificial animal'.[5] And, generally, among peoples of eastern Africa who have long been trading with the Arab world, the idea of God as distinct from the shades was more clearly developed than it was among peoples of the central interior and the south, who long remained isolated.

[1] Hunter, pp. 298-9. The word for twins in Xhosa, *ama-wele*, shows an interesting resemblance to the Luyia word for God, *Wele*. G. Wagner, 'The Abaluyia of Kavirondo', in D. Forde (ed.), *African Worlds*, (London, 1954), p. 28.

[2] The Rev. Canon Callaway, *The Religious System of the Amazulu* (Cape Town and London, 1870), pp. 1-25; M. Wilson, *Communal Rituals*, pp. 156-9; Hunter, pp. 269-70; D. Forde (ed.), *African Worlds*, p. 44.

[3] M. Wilson, *Rituals of Kinship*, pp. 4, 108, 212.

[4] J. V. Taylor, *The Primal Vision* (London, 1963), pp. 83-96.

[5] Evans-Pritchard, *Nuer Religion*, pp. 272ff., 280-2; Lienhardt, p. 153.

The third element in traditional religion was the belief that power resided in certain material substances which were mainly vegetable, but which included human flesh and blood. It was thought that those who had the knowledge manipulated these substances for both good and evil purposes. The miraculous substances are spoken of in English as 'medicines' or 'fetishes', but the translation is inevitably bad, because no parallel concept exists in contemporary Western society. 'Medicines' in Africa were thought to secure power, health, fertility, personality, or moral reform; they might be used to heal or deliberately to kill, to make a bride 'patient and polite' to her in-laws, a chief 'majestic', or a judge 'compliant'. A Nyakyusa layman's view of 'medicines' was comparable to that of an Englishman's view of atomic energy: useful but horribly dangerous.

Health, fertility, and success were thought of as controlled not only by the shades but also through medicines, as already defined. Possession of the right medicines, and sometimes the right spell to utter, was thought to give men power. There was no such thing as chance in the traditional view and differences in fortune were attributed partly to medicines.

Medicines might be used legitimately for health or defence, but often they were thought to embody a selfish seeking for power at someone else's expense, such as securing fertility by attracting it from a neighbour's field – 'over-stepping' her in Nyakyusa idiom or 'over-reaching' her we might say in English.

Medicines were not necessarily traditional: new substances were constantly sought, and in the changing societies medicines are put to new uses, such as success in passing examinations, in competitive concerts, in rugby football matches, in attracting custom, in securing employment, or (in South Africa) escaping a police raid for passes.

The belief in medicines was based on association – a feeling of likeness between things – and the likeness was taken as a causal connection. What to a modern westerner is a poetic symbol was taken as magically potent. Clouds of smoke not only symbolized rain, but *caused* rain; woolly black clouds were like woolly black rams, and since rams fight, the ram in the homestead and the thunder clouds rising in the sky might fight also. If the homestead rams were defeated the homestead was struck by lightning, so wise men left their rams in the pasture during storms and then, if the clouds were victorious, only a ram was destroyed, and not the whole homestead. So it went on. The 'forest of symbols' proliferates.

Generally in Africa the efficacy of medicines was thought of as an independent source of power which was innate in the substances themselves. Certain medicines were used, however, in conjunction with sacrifice to the shades: an Mpondo patient was washed with the 'medicine of home' (*iyeza lasekhaya*) before an animal was slaughtered, and a new-born Nyakyusa baby was washed with a medicine representing 'the blood of the lineage', whereby legitimacy was acknowledged. This use of medicines comes close to the use of miracle-working relics in medieval Europe. Power was thought to reside in certain material substances but they derived power from their association with the dead.

The fourth element was the fear of witchcraft, of an innate power to harm. Medicines might be used for good or ill, but witchcraft was innately evil. The witch in Africa was the embodiment of evil in Africa, just as the devil was in medieval Europe.

Death, it was argued, was not natural. More often than not it caught children or young adults, and almost every death was seen as caused by some person. That person was most often thought to be a witch exercising mysterious and innate power to harm, or a sorcerer who manipulated medicines with deliberate ill intent. If the patient were to recover, the witch or sorcerer must confess and express good will, hence the torture of those accused. All this is ancient in Africa. We have precise accounts of it among the Xhosa from the survivors of a wreck in 1686,[1] and so, though it is argued that the number of accusations increased as tensions increased in a changing society, fear and accusation have long existed. The idea of witchcraft is recognition of the reality of evil: the denial of it is taken as a denial of the existence of evil.

It is anger, lust, greed, and envy which are thought to materialize as pythons, or scratching cats, or lustful baboons. Brooding anger in the heart was thought to be the root of witchcraft. And since men were aware of evil impulses in themselves they could not believe that a society without witchcraft existed. I remember a conversation with the middle-aged wife of a Nyakyusa chief in 1938. She reminded me that we had been friends for some time, and that she had told me many things. She asked what was the truth about witchcraft among white people. When I replied that few believed in it, she said sadly that I was just like other Europeans, refusing to admit the truth. *Of course* witchcraft must exist in any community. We were speaking KiNyakyusa and I realized that though the precise words for witchcraft were used the implication was 'evil doing'. To her way of thinking I was denying the existence of ill-will, envy, hate, and greed.

The particular form of witch beliefs varies with the structure of the society. Where there are rigid prohibitions on marriage within a clan or outside a colour-caste then there are stories of demon lovers who have attributes of the

[1] Moodie, *The Record*, I, 427.

prohibited category; and where the sharing of prized foods is difficult to enforce the characteristic attribute of the witch is greed (see pp. 79, 84). Witchcraft is the personification of temptation, whether sex transgression, greed, or hate. You may notice that I have slipped into the present tense. There is good reason for this. Fear of witches is still very real in Africa.

Four elements in the traditional religion of south and east African peoples have been distinguished and it will be seen that they differ in character: a cult of the shades is practised and medicines are used throughout the area, but sacrifice to God occurs sporadically, and witchcraft as distinguished from sorcery is something feared rather than practised. But in any concrete situation all four elements are commonly mentioned. On one and the same occasion men may sacrifice to the shades and use medicines; they may argue whether a misfortune has been caused by God or by a supposed witch.

What men continually sought in traditional African society – what they worshipped – was life, vitality, fertility. Life was sought from the shades, from God, or through medicines. Sometimes it was thought to be withheld or destroyed by the shades or god, or by evil men manipulating medicines of sorcery or the power of witchcraft. It could also be destroyed by pollution, which at root was a mishandling of life and potency.

Very generally in Africa it is thought that pollution comes from certain physiological conditions – birth and death, menstruation and coition, from certain medicines, from the gods, and, particularly among the Nyakyusa, from the founding heroes. The idea that *sacer* includes both the holy and the polluting is familiar enough to scholars.[1] The

[1] R. Otto, *The Idea of the Holy* (English translation J. W. Harvey, London, 1926), *passim.*

numinous was fearful in Israel as in Africa. It included, among the Nyakyusa, the fearfulness of fertility, particularly as expressed in twin-births; the fearfulness of certain medicines which were thought to be akin to witchcraft; the fearfulness of the shades, of the heroes, above all of the living representatives of the heroes, and the pythons which dwelt in their sacred groves.[1] That which was thought of as *powerful* was taken as polluting.

The pure (*mwelu*) were those who were empty (*bwasi*) and contrasted with those who were heavy (*nsito*) with the power of medicines or witchcraft, or recent sexual activity, though in certain circumstances the sex act was thought of as a purification.[2] Celibacy was not honoured in itself, but it was supposed that different sorts of potency might injure each other, as sex activity, menstruation or pregnancy, and powerful medicines. Potency and purity were opposite poles. It has indeed been argued very persuasively that the root of pollution is the mixing of things which it is felt should be kept separate.[3] This is driven to extremes in those societies in which minorities have been preoccupied with maintaining their separate identity, and not mixing with their neighbours – societies such as ancient Israel, India, and contemporary South Africa – but separating things felt to be antagonistic is a common element in avoiding pollution.

The dogmas regarding witchcraft, the shades, medicines, and pollution were the explanation of good and evil fortune, the answer to 'Why did it happen to me?'. In pagan theology

[1] M. Wilson, *Rituals of Kinship*, pp. 17, 30, 152, 219; *Communal Rituals*, pp. 28-30, 41, 44-6, 48, 60-3, 155-8.

[2] Blowing out of water, which was a symbol of getting rid of anger, was also a symbol of male emission. Both may be understood as a purging of passion. M. Wilson, *Communal Rituals*, p. 109.

[3] Mary Douglas, *Purity and Danger* (London, 1966), pp. 35, 113, *et passim*.

suffering was linked with sin – one's own sin or that of kinsmen, living and dead – or it was attributed to the malice of an enemy. Suffering was not something unaccountable or due to chance. As Geertz has argued: 'suffering due to sin is felt more tolerable than the torment of the just'.[1] Among Nyakyusa and Mpondo, and other African peoples of whom I have read, there is a deep-rooted belief in the moral order of the universe. Social life exists and chaos is controlled: the order of society and the order of the universe are linked so that wrong-doing by men is thought to bring disorder in the heavens, drought or flood, hail, or lightning which kills.

Anthropologists have been concerned to disentangle the relation between the idea of pollution and sin, and this is discussed in the chapter on morality (see pp. 79-82). Pollution among Nyakyusa or Mpondo is not thought of as directly due to sin any more than infection is with us. What is sinful is to ignore the rules regarding pollution and so injure others. I myself agree with the psychoanalysts that there is a link between concepts of pollution and a sense of guilt,[2] but often it is not direct. The Nyakyusa who washes and anoints himself repeatedly after a burial is explicitly separating himself from the corpse, and acknowledging the need to turn from death to life, and accept a change in social relationships, but I doubt whether he is conscious of any 'death wish' about which he feels guilty. Similarly the nubile girl who purifies herself is taught that neglect of the menstrual taboos may injure others, and she fears sterility herself if she neglects the ritual. She is aware that she must accept a change in status and new, very onerous, obligations as a wife; but I doubt if she is aware of guilt over the aggressions of infancy.

[1] Geertz, pp. 17-42.
[2] M. Wilson, *Rituals of Kinship*, p. 233; *Communal Rituals*, p. 161.

Purification recurs in the rituals of all the African people I know, or of whom I have read, though it is probably more emphasized among some than among others. I interpret it as a reflection, however indirect, of conflicts within individuals. This is a theme I cannot pursue because I am not trained in psychology or psychoanalysis. There is, however, an explicit connection among the Nyakyusa between getting rid of anger and purification. At every family ritual kinsmen were pressed to 'speak out', to purge themselves of anger. At a communal ritual the great men of the country were likewise required to 'speak out' (see pp. 28, 65, 89). So although pollution was not consciously thought of as being caused by sin alone, there was a direct and explicit connection between them.

That which is not seen was thought to be revealed to ordinary men through dreams, but more especially to professional diviners who acted as clairvoyants and administered oracles. Throughout Africa diviners have practised and still practise, answering the questions of their clients about the cause of disease or other misfortune, the identity of supposed witches and sorcerers, the will of the shades. As Professor Evans-Pritchard pointed out long ago, the diviner settles choices.[1] Alternative causes of courses of action are put before him by his clients – more or less directly – and he settles between them. The methods of divination are legion, ranging from administering poison to a person or a chicken, throwing bones, or dice, or noticing the spoor of animals overnight in prepared sand, to working oneself into a frenzy and pouncing on the supposed witch – 'smelling out' the culprit as the Xhosa say. In poison ordeals the innocent were thought to vomit, the guilty to die or suffer injury. Sceptics existed: as one Nyakyusa remarked to me,

[1] Evans-Pritchard, *Witchcraft*, pp. 88-9.

in a case involving the poison ordeal they always sent his sister to represent his lineage for she vomited on the slightest provocation; but criticism was commonly of particular diviners or particular techniques, rather than of divination as a method of discovering truth.

We are concerned with the sort of changes that have occurred in traditional pagan theology as African societies expanded in scale. First, the idea of personal causation of misfortune is extremely tenacious. When misfortune hits them directly men find it hard to believe in impersonal causes, or to accept any dogma of chance, but, as their society increases in scale, they begin to interpret other people's troubles, or their own lesser troubles, in impersonal terms. The field within which natural causation is accepted extends. One reflection of this is the rising attendance at hospitals and clinics in Africa: people accept the ability of the western-trained doctors to cure or alleviate many diseases, though not all disease. And in town *more* misfortunes are attributed to natural causes than in the country.[1]

Secondly, men cling to the idea of the shades, the belief that their own ancestors are particularly interested in them and a source of help in trouble. The South African writer, Ezekiel Mphahlele, noted that most of his fellow Africans, educated men and professing Christians, 'believe firmly in the spirits of their ancestors', and 'when we seek moral guidance and inspiration and hope, somewhere in the recesses of our being, we grope around for some link with these spirits'.[2] This is borne out by evidence from other sources; and with the growth of African nationalism traditional

[1] M. Wilson and A. Mafeje, *Langa* (Cape Town, 1963), pp. 110-12; W. D. Hammond-Tooke, 'Urbanization and the Interpretation of Misfortune', *Africa*, **40**, 1, (1970), p. 30.

[2] E. Mphahlele, *Down Second Avenue* (London, 1959), pp. 63-4.

beliefs in the power and righteousness of the ancestors are linked to new causes. 'The old Gods' of Africa are invoked to aid leaders against white power.[1] Belief in a moral order maintained by God and the shades is expressed by young men as well as by their elders. Ultimately, they say, the oppressor is punished. Rituals must be modified, and detached from a pastoral or agricultural economy as men move to town. Occasions of celebration continue, but imperceptibly the ritual of bringing back the shade of a father merges into a commemoration dinner; or the sacrifice of a white goat after the birth of a child into a baptism feast. Reverence for the dead continues: fear of their power over the living diminishes.

Dependence upon 'medicines' (in the particular sense defined) to control situations continues, and all sorts of new materials (such as grease from engines on the mines) are used. Murders to obtain human flesh for medicines increased in some places during the struggle between different leaders for power,[2] and I believe that the danger of such murders is still very real. There are persistent reports of contemporary rulers using medicines to bolster their position. The traditional medicines, including the ingredient of human flesh, merge into patent medicines advertised by modern commercial firms. There is one advertised in the press in South Africa as the 'powa pill', so white-owned commercial firms have entered the profitable field of magic-to-secure-power.

These problems are not new: in the fifth century A.D. St Augustine of Hippo spoke of 'People wearing amulets, assiduous clients of sorcerers and astrologers',[3] and the use

[1] Wilson and Mafeje, p. 112.

[2] G. I. Jones, *Basutoland Medicine Murder* (H.M.S.O., 1951, Cmd 8209).

[3] Peter Brown, *Augustine of Hippo* (London, 1967), p. 213.

of relics in medieval Europe was much like the African use of medicines. Possession of some substances in which mystical power was believed to reside gave greater assurance to many than prayer. A shift from the use of magic – chiefly 'medicines' or fetishes in Africa – to prayer, in the sense of inner communion with God, is the great leap in the shift from outward forms to inner religion. Some people, of course, deny that such a shift ever takes place. They view prayer as verbal magic.

Revival movements in which pagan prophets pressed their followers to renounce witchcraft and cast away dangerous medicines have been recorded in Africa since the middle of the last century. Such movements probably existed before contact with whites, for purification from witchcraft, implying purification from anger and ill-will, is one of the fundamental themes of the traditional religion. But revival movements proliferated during periods of acute tension and acquired political implications, as on the eastern Cape frontier in 1857, when the Xhosa believed their dead would rise if they purified themselves from witchcraft, and sacrificed all their cattle to the shades.

Sometimes the movement was pagan in form and the leaders were diviners of more or less traditional pattern, as in 1857 among the Xhosa, and in Zambia in the Muchapi movement of 1934.[1] But even these movements reflected messianic ideas learnt from Christian missionaries,[2] and from the 1920s in the south there have been explicitly Christian movements whose leaders preached repentance

[1] A. I. Richards, 'A Modern Movement of Witchfinders', *Africa*, **8** (1935), 448-61; M. G. Marwick, 'Another Modern Anti-Witchcraft Movement in East Central Africa', *Africa*, **20** (1950), 100-12.

[2] Wilson and Thompson, I, 256–60; M-L. Martin, *The Biblical Concept of Messianism and Messianism in the New Testament* (Morija, 1964).

and renunciation of witchcraft and medicines much as their pagan predecessors did. The most influential of these Christian prophets in recent years has been Alice Lenshina in Zambia.[1] Most Christian revival movements, like earlier pagan ones, have political overtones, and Alice Lenshina was imprisoned, and then confined to a distant area, by the Zambian government after independence.

One characteristic of the movements, common to both Christian and pagan forms, is an orgy of denunciation, neighbour accusing neighbour of practising witchcraft or sorcery, and also self-accusation, men vying with one another to admit evil doing and bring forth their instruments of sorcery.

It is curious to find evidence of a similar orgy of denunciation under the secular ideology of communism. Consider this passage from *Doctor Zhivago*: 'It was the disease, the revolutionary madness of the age; that in his heart everyone was utterly different from his words and the outward appearance he assumed. No one had a clear conscience. Everyone had some reason to fear that he was guilty of everything, that he was an impostor, an undetected criminal. The slightest pretext was enough to launch the imagination on an orgy of self-torture. People slandered and accused themselves, not only out of terror but of their own will, from a morbidly destructive impulse in a state of metaphysical trance, carried away by that passion of self-condemnation which cannot be checked once it has been given free rein.'[2] Pasternak was, after all, describing what he had seen, what he had experienced as an insider. It is an extreme example

[1] J. V. Taylor and D. Lehmann, *Christians of the Copperbelt* (London, 1961), pp. 248-67.

[2] B. Pasternak, *Doctor Zhivago*, English translation by M. Hayward and M. Harari (London, 1958), p. 409.

of what Erik Erikson describes as 'man's inner proclivity to persecute himself and thus to identify himself with his persecutor'.[1] The peculiarity is the epidemic form.

Europeans – missionaries, administrators, judges, and scholars – have very often confused diviners who are witch-finders with witches; some are still doing so.[2] This is comparable to confusing detective and criminal in terms of traditional African morality. The confusion is partly a linguistic one; in Xhosa the words for diviner and witch (*igqira* and *igqwira*) sound very similar to those unfamiliar with the language, and the abominable English word 'witch-doctor' is commonly used to mean *both* diviner and witch. Diviners are sometimes convicted of imputation of witchcraft, which was a criminal offence in all the British colonies of Africa and which remains a statutory offence in at least some of the independent African states. Missionaries argue, probably correctly, that witch-finders foster fear of witchcraft. But when outsiders identify diviner and witch, African villagers assume either crass stupidity or deliberate double talk. The assertion by whites that witchcraft does not exist, that medicines (apart from poison orally administered) are powerless, carries little conviction, for what they symbolize does exist. Anger, hate and greed are real, and men know this.

It is rather surprising that European missionaries found African ideas of witchcraft so difficult to understand because in fact they are very close to those of medieval Europe, and even in the eighteenth century John Wesley taught that to deny witchcraft was to deny the Bible. Some missionaries

[1] Erik Erikson, *Insight and Responsibility* (New York, 1964), p. 102.

[2] D. Williams, *When Races Meet* (Johannesburg, 1967), pp. 75, 81. J. H. Soga (a Xhosa speaker), who did not confuse diviner and witch, is misquoted.

thought that pagan diviners were in league with the devil; others that diviners were charlatans pretending to power they did not possess. All without exception condemned witch-finding.

Divination continues to be widely practised in traditional forms and also in forms which have been, and still are, used in Europe and America. The Old and New Testaments bear witness to the antiquity and tenacity of belief in divination and it has continued in one form or another in the Christian Church until this century. Not only did Jonah's shipmates cast lots to discover who was the cause of the storm,[1] but the Apostles cast lots to choose one to replace Judas,[2] and the lot has been repeatedly used to settle choices in the Moravian Church. The selection of candidates for baptism and ordination, and brides for missionaries, was determined by lot.[3] In the secular world it is still conventional to flick a coin to settle which team will open the batting, but not considered proper to choose a bride in this way.

It was noted earlier that the idea of God was elaborated in some parts of Africa, and was elsewhere scarcely discernible. Whether it was clear or hazy traditionally, it is readily accepted in the changing society, and the shades are spoken of as intermediaries between men and God. Educated Africans now commonly argue that the conception of God was always clear among them and the shades were always intermediaries. As I said, I question whether evidence from the first period of interaction between white and African in Zululand or BuNyakyusa supports this, but the current interpretation of past ideas is plain. There is a splendid

[1] Jonah 1:7.
[2] Acts 1:26.
[3] B. Krüger, *The Pear Tree Blossoms* (Genadendal, 1968), pp. 32, 34, 40, 48, 57-8, 81-2, 87, 120, 149, 172, 182, 208-10, 226.

assertion of it by my friend the Rev. Gabriel Setiloane.[1] The idea of God is nowhere rejected: it is *added* to ideas about the shades, witchcraft, and medicines, and since the shades were senior kinsmen the concept of God as Father is not foreign: it is part of the ancient tradition.[2] But some of the imagery changes. Where God was scarcely distinguished from the shades he was thought of as being beneath the earth as they were, but as he is more clearly distinguished he goes up-stairs and dwells above. I heard this happening over twenty years ago among the Nyakyusa in Tanzania. In 1935 old men – pagans – spoke of God beneath: young men – pagans – were beginning to speak of him as dwelling above as the Christians did. By 1955 the shift was complete, and to young and old, pagan and Christian alike, God dwelt on high.[3]

The radical change is not the addition of an idea of God or the spatial symbols men use regarding him, but the shift to monotheism when God alone is thought to create life, and to an incarnation in which God himself is thought to suffer. Recently an African priest writing to other Africans added to his commentary: 'The resurrection involved the gift of life, a prerogative belonging solely to God.' An English priest might have taken the second statement for granted and not added it.

A second radical shift is in the conception of life. Small-scale societies are preoccupied with reproduction. Necessarily they are so preoccupied because physical survival in a small group with limited tools and knowledge was difficult. The modern citizen of a rich nation need no longer struggle

[1] Gabriel Setiloane, 'Frontier Meditation' ,*Frontier*, February 1969, pp. 19-22.

[2] Cf. J. B. Danquah, *The Akan Doctrine of God* (1944, 2nd ed. London, 1968), pp. 23-4.

[3] M. Wilson, *Communal Rituals*, pp. 157-9.

to survive and reproduce, but some of his values belong to the period when he was obliged so to struggle. In the Christian tradition the stress changes from survival to quality of life. Eternal life is interpreted as beginning here and now and consisting essentially in a quality of life. I think this was apprehended by most Nyakyusa converts to Christianity who, though unsophisticated villagers, when asked why they had become Christians replied unhesitatingly 'because there is life'.

Thirdly, God becomes approachable. In the pagan tradition in much of Africa, as in Israel, what was stressed was the awfulness of God. In Nyakyusa thought a man who came too close to the gods went mad, and rituals were directed towards driving them off. The source of fecundity was fearful and contaminating: spiritual power was the *opposite* of innocence and purity. Enoch who walked with God[1] was a stranger in Africa. So one of the radical changes as Africans turn to Christianity is the seeking for union with God, rather than separation from that which is powerful and dangerous.

The fourth and greatest change lies in the conception that suffering somehow may be creative: that men participate in God's activity through the acceptance of suffering.

Suffering remains a mystery.[2] Men continue to ask why it exists if God be good. Why are some afflicted and not others? The small pagan societies had clear-cut answers to this: they linked suffering directly with sin. Even physical evil such as drought and flood was attributed to sin: neglect of mourning taboos was thought to lead to parched fields and pasture among the Tswana,[3] insult to the senior priest of the

[1] Genesis 5:24.

[2] Cf. H. A. Williams, *The Suffering of Mankind* (address in Coventry Cathedral, 5th Dec. 1966).

[3] J. T. Brown, *Among the Bantu Nomands* (London, 1926), pp. 130-1; B. A. Pauw, *Religion in a Tswana Chiefdom* (Cape Town, 1960), pp. 24-8.

country to flood among the Nyakyusa.[1] Lightning was thought to strike those who quarrelled with neighbours, for it was believed to be controlled by certain skilled men who, for a consideration, would blast a particular individual. The victim was thought unfortunate but the wise did not excite enmity. He who walked humbly might hope never to arouse such vindictiveness.

Some professing Christians continue to link all misfortune – even physical evil such as an earthquake or drought – with sin. But those who are steeped in the New Testament as well as the Book of Job cannot do so. What we can *see* is suffering transmuted in love in a life of service and sometimes in creation.[2] When God is believed to suffer he redeems suffering, and so enables men who are asking 'Why did it happen to me?' to ask instead: 'What can be created out of this suffering?'.

There is another idea, very difficult to define, but fundamental to an understanding of the difference between small- and large-scale societies. In the rituals of small societies, the particular and material is dominant. A celebration must be carried out in a particular manner, at a particular time, in a particular place, or it is thought to be ineffective. In an Mpondo sacrifice a cow or an ox with specified marking was killed in a prescribed manner, in the late afternoon, in the cattle-byre, by the senior man of the lineage. It had to bellow and fall in a specified way. Certain portions of meat were given to certain people. The patient on whose behalf the animal was killed ate in a prescribed fashion. Each detail was held to be necessary to the success of the

[1] M. Wilson, *Communal Rituals*, pp. 116-20.

[2] A contemporary example is found in the writings of Alexander Solzhenitzyn, who himself believes that 'good literature arises out of pain'; cf. Pavel Licko, 'A Visit to Solzhenitzyn', *The Listener*, 20 March 1969.

ritual as a whole. The detail prescribed varied somewhat from one lineage to another but authority for the variation was always given as received custom in that lineage, or the specific vision of a diviner. The inward and spiritual attitudes of the participants were not wholly irrelevant – if kinsmen were quarrelling, if a senior were still angry, the sick man for whom the ritual was celebrated might not recover. But efficacy was thought to lie in particular materials manipulated in a set fashion.

There is a contrast with rituals celebrated in the Christian Church in which inward and spiritual attitudes are asserted to be dominant, and the particular forms no more than symbols. Intrinsic quality is not inevitably contained in particular acts: the 'outward and visible sign'. All Christian rituals can be interpreted in magical fashion, and perhaps few individuals and no community of Christians is wholly free from magical attitudes – a reliance on the particular and material, a confidence that efficacy lies in certain words or substances. Relics were often used as magic in medieval Europe and were destroyed at the Reformation for that reason. But there is an enormous difference in emphasis between isolated pagan communities and Christian communities with which I have been familiar. The Christian is struggling to 'worship Him in spirit and in truth'.[1] The record of the gradual separation of inward attitudes from material forms in ancient Israel is there in the Old Testament,[2] and it continues through the history of the Church. The present process of secularization is, in part, a rejection of magical attitudes, an attempt to free the spirit from particular ritual forms no longer felt to be relevant.

[1] John 4:24.

[2] E.g. 1 Samuel 15:22, 'behold, to obey is better than sacrifice, and to harken than the fat of rams'.

It has been argued in this chapter that the traditional religions of southern and eastern Africa involved four elements: a cult of the shades, belief in God, belief in the power of 'medicines', and fear of witchcraft. Men sought life and fertility from the shades and from God, and through medicines; they thought it could be destroyed directly by the shades, more rarely by God, but that most often it was destroyed by evil men using evil medicines – sorcery – or witchcraft, or through pollution which came from the mishandling of potency. That which was powerful was taken as polluting. Good and evil fortune were explained in terms of these beliefs and suffering linked with sin. The universe was conceived as being orderly and moral. Certain men and women practised as diviners, or clairvoyants; they were thought to reveal the will of the shades – sometimes even of God – and divination was used to discover the causes of misfortune, and to settle choices.

With change in scale has gone a development of the idea of God, a ready acceptance of it in those parts where the idea was shadowy, and for some people a shift to monotheism. God becomes more approachable – the awfulness of the powerful is less – and the conception of life changes. But the shades are still invoked by many people; they are thought of as intermediaries between man and God. The idea of personal causation of misfortune is tenacious, and divination is still used to discover the cause of misfortune and to settle choices. 'Witch-finding' often takes the form of a revival movement. Belief in a fundamental moral order is reasserted but misfortune is not so closely linked to sin as in the dogmas of the traditional societies, and the idea that suffering can be creative appears. As scale extends, intrinsic quality is thought of as relatively separate from particular acts: rites are taken as symbolic rather than magical.

III. RITUAL AND SYMBOLISM

In all societies men express themselves in symbols. In literate societies speech and writing predominate: in pre-literate societies other symbols are relatively more important. As Marett argued, preliterate men *dance* their religion rather than formulating dogmas.[1] Although there is no sharp cleavage between societies in this regard there is a difference in emphasis. In most small societies elaborate funeral rites, initiation or marriage rites, and first fruits rites are celebrated; they may last for weeks; but there are no creeds or schools of theology. In the large societies rituals are attenuated but theological debate proliferates.

Myths are often associated with the rituals of small societies – myths of the origin of man and of animals, of fire, crops, chieftainship, and ritual itself. The myths provide a charter for the social structure and perhaps a just-so story explaining the origin of the ritual, but it is the dramatic presentation, not the intellectual argument, that is stressed.

Religion is not confined in ritual, but it is manifest in ritual, and in the smallest societies chiefly manifest in ritual. Indeed, nineteenth-century travellers and missionaries often denied that the peoples they visited had any religion at all because they could not discover any body of dogma relating to God, only what they perceived as 'heathen' customs and dances.[2]

As societies grow in scale they become more specialized

[1] R. R. Marett, *The Threshold of Religion* (London, 2nd edition, 1911), p. 180.

[2] Robert Moffat, *Missionary Labours and Scenes in Southern Africa* (London, 1842), pp. 244, 251, 257-68.

and, as was argued earlier, secularization is one aspect of specialization.

In the small society religious rituals are closely integrated with everyday economic and political activities; in the large society these become more and more separate. As societies grow in scale the political leader is no longer the religious leader, nor are crops and herds thought to depend directly on his health and behaviour. Even the various forms of artistic expression are secularized. Carving, sculpture, painting, drama, and dancing become separated from specifically religious ritual, though they are used in ritual.

The symbolic patterns of a society vary with the social structure; that is, the manner in which a people conceives of reality, and their relation to it is connected with the kinship, economic, and political structures, though not wholly determined by them. There is a *relative* autonomy between the different aspects. A number of anthropologists, notably Professor Evans-Pritchard and Dr Godfrey Lienhardt of Oxford, and Dr Mary Douglas of London have demonstrated the close link between men's classification of natural phenomena, and their social structure.[1] Dr Lienhardt describes how, among the Dinka cattle-herders of the Sudan, cattle represent human relationships, the young circumcised men identifying themselves with their oxen. 'The Dinka's very perception of colour, light and shade in the world around them is . . . inextricably connected with their recognition of colour-configurations in cattle.'[2] The Lele, who are hunters and cultivators living on the fringe of the Congo forests,

[1] E. E. Evans-Pritchard, *Theories of Primitive Religion* (Oxford, 1965), p. 58 (referring to Australian material).

[2] Lienhardt, pp. 12-13.

divide their world into forest and grass land, identifying the first with male, the second with female.[1]

Symbolic patterns in the societies that have been studied in Africa all deny chaos, and depict a meaning in life. As I said in the previous chapter, suffering was linked with wrong-doing and so made meaningful and endurable. Misfortune was commonly attributed to a man's own wrong-doing; sometimes to that of his ancestors or kinsmen; sometimes to the malice of an enemy. But even where he was thought to suffer from the witchcraft or sorcery – that is, the malice of a neighbour, a spouse, co-wife, a former lover, or even a kinsman – the attack was in some sense regarded as the victim's own fault, for the moral code required that he should not quarrel with these people. If he lived in love and charity with them, as he should, then he would be safe. (We shall return to this point in the chapter on morality.)

The symbolism of another society must be translated systematically not guessed at. Guessing the meaning of symbolic action in a strange culture is comparable to guessing the meaning of words in a strange language: a few are immediately intelligible; most are not. The translation depends on discovering the more and the less conscious association made by participants, and this involves a deep knowledge of language, gesture, and categories of thought. The associations made by participants (i.e. their translation of a ritual) is not the full analysis of any ritual. I have never been so stupid as to suppose so,[2] though I have been accused of

[1] M. Douglas, 'The Lele of the Kasai' in D. Forde (ed.), *African Worlds*, pp. 4-7.

[2] M. Wilson, *Rituals of Kinship*, p. 6: 'The interpretations of even the most self-conscious Nyakyusa, such as Kasitile the rain-maker, Mwandisi the old blind historian, Mwasalemba, Lyandileko and Kakune the doctors, do not, of course, reveal the whole truth about Nyakyusa rituals, but *any analysis not based on some translation of the symbols used* by people of that culture is open to suspicion.'

saying this.[1] The old serve as Aunt Sallies for their successors to shy at, and if Sally is erected crooked she topples the more easily. But the translation of symbolism is a necessary first step in any study of ritual, and a first step that has very often been neglected. The outsider guesses and tells his reader what he supposes the participants mean. Theories of ritual based on guesswork are still being produced, but we have now in Africa what might be called dictionaries of symbolism for a number of peoples. Detailed analyses of ritual and symbolism have been published for Bemba, Ndembu, and Lele in Central Africa; Nyakyusa, Gogo, and Kaguru in Tanzania; Lugbara in Uganda; and Dinka and Nuer in the Sudan; and various groups in West Africa.[2]

An interpreter takes the student of these peoples by the hand, as the Interpreter guided Pilgrim in Bunyan's parable three centuries ago.

Symbols are rooted in the common biological nature of man – male and female, birth, death, mating, menstruation, pregnancy, suckling, sickness; elimination, and so forth;

[1] M. Gluckman (ed.), *Closed Systems and Open Minds* (Edinburgh 1964), pp. 37-8; V. W. Turner, *The Forest of Symbols* (Ithaca, 1967), p. 34.

[2] Richards, *Chisungu*; V. W. Turner, *The Drums of Affliction* (Oxford, 1968); *Forest of Symbols*; M. Douglas, 'The Lele of the Kasai'; M. Wilson, *Rituals of Kinship*; *Communal Rituals*; P. Rigby, 'Dual Symbolic Classification among the Gogo of Central Tanzania', *Africa*, **36,** 1 (1966), 1-17; 'Some Gogo Rituals of Purification' in *Dialectic in Practical Religion*, edited E. R. Leach (Cambridge, 1968); 'The Structural Context of Girls' Puberty Rites', *Man*, **2,** 3 (1967), 434-44; T. O. Beidelman, 'Three Tales of the Living and the Dead', *Journal of the Royal Anthropological Institute*, **94,** 2 (1964), 109-37; 'Right and Left Hand among the Kaguru', *Africa* **31,** 3 (1961), 250-7; 'Pig (Guluwe): An essay on Ngulu Sexual Symbolism and Ceremony', *Southwestern Journal of Anthropology*, **20,** 4 (1964), 359-92; J. Middleton, *Lugbara Religion* (London, 1960); Lienhardt; Evans-Pritchard, *Nuer Religion*; M. Griaule, *Masques Dogons* (Paris, 1938); G. Dieterlin, *Les Âmes des Dogons* (Paris, 1941).

in the physical structure of the universe – the seasons, the waxing and waning of the moon, drought and flood, and in the local environment. The same social conflicts within men and between men, such as ambivalent attitudes towards incest, parental authority, and birth and death, are repeatedly represented; and the conception of pollution, which constantly recurs, as constantly has a physiological reference.[1] But the particular symbols used for man and woman, birth and death, anger and forgiveness, vary. They vary like language from one culture to another. There tends to be a similarity of symbol in the same language-family (as through Bantu-speaking Africa), but this is modified by economy. As a young anthropologist I worked first among a cattle people, the Mpondo of the Transkei, and then I moved to a banana people, the Nyakyusa of Tanzania. Their symbols differed greatly though they both spoke Bantu languages, and lived as cultivators and stock keepers.[2] The Nyakyusa pictured men and women, death, and the proliferating lineage in terms of plantains and sweet bananas; the Mpondo in terms of cattle. English was totally inadequate to translate the rich vocabulary relating to bananas in KiNyakyusa, or cattle in IsiMpondo: even the distinctions made in type of plantain or cattle could not be translated, much less the symbolic reference.

Throughout Africa there are altars – traditional places for sacrifice. But as was noted earlier, the location of the family altar, as well as the kind of sacrificial offering, varies with the economy, from the cattle-byre of the Xhosa or Dinka, to the

[1] Douglas, *Purity and Danger*, p. 120.

[2] According to tradition cattle were brought to the Nyakyusa valley by the ancestors of the chiefs ten generations before 1935, in fact (calculating from radiocarbon dates) in the early fifteenth century; but the symbolism of KiNyakyusa is still dominated by bananas rather than cattle.

banana grove of Nyakyusa and Ganda, and the forked branch or tree, decorated with trophies of the chase among a people who depended upon hunting like the Ndembu. And the place of sacrifice for the community as a whole may be a pool or a grove associated with the shades, a high mountain, a tree identified with that mountain, or a particular species of tree symbolizing motherhood and matriliny.

It is likely that some symbols are constant, such as serpents and fire for sex, but the same symbol may have many associations and some of them are not constant. I find that the python is a symbol for *ultimate* power down the eastern side of Africa from the Sudan to the Cape, but it is hardly that in Christian Europe. A most striking contrast is in the moral qualities associated with the wild and the tame, the bush and the village. Among the Anuak the wild is holy, but among the nearby Dinka it is the village which is moral.[1] There is a similar contrast for the pygmies of the Ituri forest and the villagers who live there.[2]

The symbols used in ritual are public not private. Their function is to communicate, and in small societies they are often directly demonstrated with models or diagrams at initiation rituals.[3] They may coincide with private symbols revealed in psychoanalysis, and indeed, individuals dream in the symbols of their society, as they think in the categories of their own language. But private imaginings go beyond the set forms. We all make particular associations with a given form, or sound, or scent which is rooted in our private experience. Occasionally the private experience takes shape in

[1] Lienhardt, p. 159.

[2] C. M. Turnbull, *Wayward Servants* (London, 1966), pp. 14-15.

[3] Richards, *Chisungu*; A. R. W. Crosse-Upcott, 'The Social Structure of the KiNgindo-speaking Peoples' (unpublished Ph.D. thesis, University of Cape Town, 1955).

poem or picture, and 'catches on', because it expresses what others feel in a way they find appropriate. Some individuals in every society have a wider symbolic perception than others, and as one learns another language, or studies the rituals of another people, one's symbolic vocabulary is enlarged. This is often very exciting, for it increases understanding of ourselves. It is one reason why we anthropologists delight in studying ritual. But here we are concerned only with public ritual; the forms given and recognized in a particular society.

Rituals compel expression of certain attitudes. Whatever a pagan Nyakyusa widow might feel she was *required* to express extravagant grief at her husband's funeral. And a woman who bore twins was required to avoid her fellows, and was avoided by them. I asked a Christian Nyakyusa whether Christians who ignored the twin ritual did not fear as pagans did. She replied: 'What she thinks in her heart I do not see; what I think in my heart you cannot see, but we do see that no-one avoids her.'[1]

Individuals or groups may rebel if what they are required to express seems to them too far from reality. This happened a hundred years ago on what was then the frontier in South Africa, when a group of white Christians refused to take communion with their coloured neighbours.[2] That reluctance is still constantly visible. The expression of brotherhood in the communion ritual is felt by some white South Africans to be too far from the reality of daily life to observe, and too dangerous to ignore, since it may compel a change in everyday life.

Rituals arouse emotion and canalize it. They occur in *all* societies, not only in the small societies we have noted, at the

[1] M. Wilson, *Communal Rituals*, p. 174.
[2] Williams, pp. 199-200.

crises of life: birth, marriage, death, and often as a celebration of maturity for an adolescent. For the community as a whole they are commonly celebrated at seedtime and at harvest, before and after battle, and at a coronation or change in government. They occur, then, when individuals and groups are excited and they provide an obligatory form for expressing their emotion.

Beneath this level rituals fulfil a necessary function. They provide a form for acting out conflicting emotions, ambivalent desires. In Nyakyusa ritual the participants act out both what they want to happen and what they do not want to happen. These last are referred to as the actions of a madman, and the explicit purpose of the Nyakyusa rituals was given, again and again, as being action 'to prevent people going mad'. The mourners for whom no rite was celebrated, or the parents of twins, or a nubile girl left to adjust themselves alone, desperately feared madness. Acting out conflicting emotions helps to make them conscious and it has been shown that, at least in 1935, many Nyakyusa were conscious of the anti-social attitudes which the rituals compelled the participant to express and reject.[1] In the political sphere, in a ritual to purify the chiefdom at the break of the rains, men actually *fought*, and sang: 'Let us dance, let us fight that the homestead may be peaceful.'[2] Similarly at a funeral or a birth ritual the kinsmen who gathered were pressed to speak out and express any quarrels and mutual criticisms they had in order that they might be reconciled, one with another.

They both admitted their former anger, one with another, and asserted that they were now in love and charity. I once

[1] M. Wilson, *Rituals of Kinship*, pp. 48-62, 67-85, 166-71.

[2] M. Wilson, *Communal Rituals*, p. 104. A South African comments: 'cf. an inter-varsity rugby match'.

watched a child of four who had been greatly angered by an adult, a stranger to him, miming that adult and making fun of him. This happened some days after the quarrel and the insulting phrase which had so angered the child was repeated. The child was an English-speaking South African but I was reminded irresistibly of Nyakyusa ritual. The child acted out a remembered conflict.

As Dr Leach has said: 'ritual makes explicit and conscious those powerful and dangerous thoughts which are liable to become repressed'.[1] This is what gives them their bite. Rituals recall individual experience and link what is sub-conscious, or only partly conscious, with the values of the society. Victor Turner shows that: 'At one pole the references are grossly, even blatantly, physiological; at the other, ideals and moral imperatives, as well as social rules, may be presented . . . It is as though the whole strength of the emotion aroused by the ideas culturally associated with the organic reference of such symbols is borrowed, as it were, by the normative and ethical reference.'[2]

The symbol is a flower, rooted in the earth of physiological processes, and the flower represents some aspect of morality. This was plain enough in Greek drama where the incest theme gradually became more and more explicit. *Oedipus Rex* was a religious ritual when it was first enacted; even now, when it is acted as a secular drama, it continues to fulfil its function of making men more conscious of conflicts within themselves.

I have referred to individual experience, but the anthropologist is not competent to analyse the roots of emotion in

[1] E. R. Leach, 'Magical Hair', *Journal of the Royal Anthropological Institute*, **88**, 11 (1958), p. 161; cf. V. W. Turner, *The Ritual Process* (Chicago, 1969), p. 25.

[2] Turner, *Drums of Affliction*, p. 18.

individuals. Nor is the psychiatrist competent to analyse the symbolic idiom of a culture with which he is not familiar. Any full and comparative study of ritual must therefore turn on cooperation between scholars trained in different disciplines or, more rarely, on an individual prepared to spend a lifetime qualifying in several fields. I think of the joint work of Meyer and Doris Fortes as an example of fruitful cooperation,[1] and that of M. J. Field[2] who draws on training in anthropology, medicine, psychiatry, and linguistics. As anthropologists we are concerned with the forms set by the society, but we know very well that what weight they carry must depend in some measure on individual experience.

The ethologists have recently shown that formalized behaviour which they call ritual may become innate in animals or birds. They are, in fact, busy defining how far it is innate and how far learnt, and at what precise stage the learning can occur, for if the animal or bird does not see the display or hear the song at the right stage it will never learn at all. The parallel in man is the creation of habits, patterns of thought and action, which again are most effective when learnt very early.

What ethologists call ritual resembles what anthropologists call ritual in that it is symbolic and its function is to communicate.[3] Among animals it operates to limit aggression within the species. It also serves to hold a group together and distinguish it from another group. These functions are partly fulfilled in human society by what the anthropologist would

[1] Doris and Meyer Fortes, 'Psychosis and Social Change among the Tallensi of Northern Ghana', *Cahiers d'Etudes Africaines*, **21,** VI (1966).

[2] M. J. Field, *Search for Security* (London, 1960).

[3] E. R. Leach, 'A Discussion on Ritualization of Behaviour in Animals and Man', *Philosophical Transactions of the Royal Society* (London,1966), B.772, vol. 251.

call manners or rules of procedure. I think of the Nyakyusa who, when I first knew them, were a spear-happy people among whom every man went armed. The obligatory greeting, in daily use, took several minutes. I embarked on it once with a Nyakyusa-speaker, in a ground-floor entrance hall at the University of Cape Town; when I had climbed three stories the formal phrases were still echoing up and down the stair-well, as yet incomplete. Parliamentary and diplomatic procedures likewise delay the approach of opponents; bowing, curtseying, and kneeling to greet (as was customary in parts of Africa) express deference, much as the gander expresses it. Above all, laughter, 'holy laughter', replaces a threatening movement in animals. All this the ethologists refer to as ritual. But here the word is used in a much narrower sense. In this book ritual is limited to the symbolic enactment of relationships between man and what is conceived of as transcendental reality. The conception of ultimate reality may be transcendental: it may be thought of as God, or as the shades, or other spirits. Or it may be conceived of as some ultimate necessity: 'the dialectic of history', or the 'destiny' of a given race to rule. In the first chapter I said that I would use *ideology* for ultimate beliefs and values which deny the existence of transcendental reality. By this definition a Nuremberg rally, or a May Day review in Red Square are not 'ritual' in the same sense as a church service or the circumcision of Xhosa youths. And I distinguish between rituals which have a transcendental reference and ceremonials which do not. This distinction has not been generally accepted by my colleagues, but I cling to it. It is important to the anthropologist to see the parallel between transcendental rituals and those thought of as celebrating the 'destiny' of a nation in terms of a necessary historical process. Celebration at the Voortrekker Monument, near Pretoria, combines prayer to God and assertions about the destiny of the white race. Distinction between transcendental and secular elements has, indeed, difficulties because the notion of a 'master race' goes far beyond science, and so, too, does belief in the dialectic of history, and a coming classless society, but the transcendental ritual has one distinguishing mark: it is celebrated in the expectation of a response from beyond that which men see. It is expected that 'the shades' will *act*: being satisfied they will bless the initiate. And those of us who, as Christians, take communion bread and wine, believe we experience a response, or rather we respond to an initiative from outside ourselves.

In an attempt to understand the intrinsic nature of ritual I ask myself three questions: What are the occasions of ritual; what is expressed; and what are the effects of celebration? A cross-cultural study in eastern and southern Africa shows a marked consistency in both occasion and content and I think you will find considerable consistency with Christian Europe also. Of the effects of ritual we still have little systematic evidence: only scattered observations.

As has already been indicated, the occasions of ritual in Africa are the crises in the life of the individual and for the community. Division of time into weeks with a day of worship seems to have roots in the Middle East and is, perhaps, linked with markets. It does not occur in the large parts of Africa which had no regular markets until a hundred years ago or less. It is also linked with the range of relationship in time, as we shall see.

What is expressed in ritual includes first, transition, the acknowledgement of a change in status. The new-born infant is acknowledged as a member of a family and lineage; the mother of a first child, or of twins, as a person of a different category from a childless woman or one who has never borne twins; the dead man is sent off on his way as an honoured guest and ritual celebrated to ensure his reception in the world of the shades; the chief mourners (widow, widower, parent, child, or sibling) move into a new category of those-who-have-been-bereaved of a spouse, parent, child or sibling, and from whom an adjustment in relationship is required. Initiation and marriage celebrate transition to maturity. Transition is marked by a symbolic death and rebirth, sometimes quite explicit. Among the Nyakyusa the chief mourners also die:[1] they must realize death and accept it, not washing, shaving, or anointing themselves, for the dead are 'brooding over' them and they *must not* drive them off. Then they turn again to life, washing and shaving, and separating themselves from the dead. The Nyakyusa widow, having wept, is pressed to put her grief behind her and turn again to life. The dirges change to dance rhythms and the same friends who urged her to weep, now urge her to drive away dreams of the dead, and look to her children and her husband's heir who will father them.

As van Gennep, with brilliant intuition, showed fifty years ago, transition is marked again and again by rituals of separation from the old life, a period of seclusion, and reintegration into the new world. Rituals celebrated for the community also mark change in the seasons, and transition from hunger to plenty, peace to war, from one reign to another. In some societies (though not those with which we are immediately concerned) time is cut into sections by ritual. Aldous Huxley once remarked that time was intoler-

[1] M. Wilson, *Rituals of Kinship*, pp. 48-63 *et passim*; cf. A.-I. Berglund, 'Fasting and Cleansing Rites' in *Concepts of Death and Funeral Rites* (Report on the Missiological Institute, Umpumulo, Natal, 1968).

able to men unless it was divided up,[1] but this depends on how men view it. As has been shown, the conception of time is linked to the structure of society, and small groups with a shallow time depth do not in fact, cut up time in the way in which larger societies with a greater time depth do. As once isolated societies enter relations with the outside world the conception of a week (with five or seven days) is accepted readily and immediately.

Secondly, the rituals express dependence. In the African societies with which we are concerned it is dependence on kinsmen, both living and dead, and on the chief and his ancestors, which is stressed. Kinsmen are members one of another and what affects one may affect all. Senior kinsmen and chiefs are priests, and control health, and fertility, and rain. Cooperation in practical affairs and in religion is between kinsmen, fellow villagers, members of an age-group, and members of a chiefdom.

The third value stressed in the rituals is reconciliation between fellow citizens of various categories; between rulers; between chief and people; and above all, between kinsmen. If there is anger in their hearts the rituals may be ineffective. So, repeatedly, in the rituals there is confession of anger, of quarrels, and a rejection of anger, symbolized, as I have said, by blowing out water.

While admitting their anger the kinsmen or chiefs and priests should eat and drink together, sharing the offering to the shades. And among the Nyakyusa, at least, it was recognized that if men drank deeply they were more likely to speak their minds. Among the Nyakyusa where a man

[1] Aldous Huxley, *Beyond the Mexique Bay* (1934, Penguin ed. 1955), p. 151: 'any possible conception of time entails the recognition and intimate realization of the flux of perpetual perishing; and to be made aware of flux . . . is intolerable . . . The endless continuity of time is appalling; arbitrarily, therefore, men parcel up the flux into sections.'

lived with age-mates, not kinsmen, his neighbours were required to share the meat and beer if the ritual were a reconciliation with an erring son, for had he not also offended them, his father's neighbours?

Fourthly, the rituals express mutual sympathy and comfort in extremity. Kinsmen and neighbours must mourn and rejoice with one another. 'We have piped unto you and ye would not dance; we have mourned unto you and ye have not lamented',[1] is the cry of one to whom sympathy is denied. Burying a man is interpreted as a symbol of caring. Traditionally, the obligation to bury was an onerous one, laid on specific kinsmen, and in the changing society the fact that a municipality or an employer may be expected to bury one is sometimes cited as evidence that *someone* has responsibility to show care. I have heard a pagan Xhosa cite as the ultimate proof that someone was blessed: 'Jesus Christ will bury you.' The basic insecurity of men comes, not from poverty, but the feeling that no one cares about them.[2]

Fifthly, rituals reflect a social order with a hierarchy of rights and obligations. In the African societies we have been considering, rituals reflect rights of precedence in the family and chiefdom, and respect for seniors. They also reflect the bridling of power, and symbolically reject selfish 'overstepping' or over-reaching[3] of others. At one ritual involving the great men of the country a commoner priest suddenly asserted the commoners' power *vis à vis* chiefs: 'If we please we can give the chiefs worms.' This was aimed not at the ruling chief but at Kasitile, a priest of the royal line who was the great rainmaker. The reply came from the ruling chief,

[1] Matthew 11:17.

[2] T. Ingram-Smith, 'The Trouble Behind the Trouble', *The Listener*, January 1967.

[3] Literally 'over-stepping' in Nyakyusa and Xhosa.

reminding the commoners that fertility came from the chiefs living and dead. They were gathered in the homestead of the rain priest where his father was buried, and the chief exclaimed: 'Where do we look? Here is our earth . . . here is our fertility of the soil.'[1]

Order consists in not mixing what should be kept apart, and the rules of Leviticus are cited as an expression of the victory of order over chaos.[2] As indicated in Chapter II, I believe that such divisive symbols are elaborated where a group fears lest it be submerged by its neighbours, and it is no accident that the Hebrew symbolism is so readily borrowed by whites in South Africa and the American South. Chaos is pictured as the failure to maintain separation between groups. Most of Africa has not been preoccupied with separation between the cloven-footed and those that divide not the hoof,[3] or shades of complexion. In Africa it was the separation of the generations, especially the sexual activities of successive generations, and the separation of different sorts of creation or fertility that was symbolized.

The focus was on fertility. What was worshipped in the pagan groups I have studied was not society, as Durkheim supposed, but procreative power; and that power was not something left to grow wild; it was tamed and controlled. Births were carefully spaced and the virginity of a girl guarded. Under appropriate conditions the sex act was a sacrament, identified with confession of anger and purification; the coming together of husband and wife was a reconciliation, symbolically and actually.[4] As noted earlier, twins represented a fearful fecundity. Attitudes towards them

[1] M. Wilson, *Communal Rituals*, p. 137.
[2] Douglas, *Purity and Danger*, pp. 35-57.
[3] Leviticus 11:2-47.
[4] M. Wilson, *Communal Rituals*, pp. 108-10, 160-1.

were ambivalent; they were abnormal and also dangerous, in some areas too dangerous to live.[1]

Fertility was the dominant value of many societies seeking to maintain themselves where disease was uncontrolled and survival difficult. That did not include *all* small-scale societies – it did not include Tikopia for example – but survival was difficult in the greater part of Africa. Preoccupation with fertility is out of date in an age of population explosion, but it is only with difficulty that values and rituals are modified to fit the new circumstances.

Anthropologists have limited evidence about the effect of the celebration of rituals on social relations. We are not competent to study the inner effect on individuals of mourning rites, or of undergoing an initiation ritual. That is the field of psychology. But we can take note when relationships, as expressed in word and action, change after a celebration. For example, a Xhosa youth who has been circumcised is *expected* to change radically in behaviour and to begin acting responsibly as a man, immediately he emerges from seclusion. In the country he still commonly does so, but there is a constant complaint in Langa, a suburb of Cape Town, that youths circumcised there do not change their habits; they continue to behave irresponsibly.[2] What of the effect of other rituals? Professor Victor Turner has done most work on this, and he has shown how, in specific cases among the Ndembu, celebrations of ritual brought conflicts within the village into the open, and achieved some measure of reconciliation between the contending parties.[3] To take

[1] M. Wilson, *Rituals of Kinship*, pp. 152-71.
[2] Wilson and Mafeje, p. 108.
[3] Turner, *Forest of Symbols*, pp. 388-93; *Drums of Affliction*, pp. 172-3, 191-7.

another example, in BuNyakyusa, between 1935 and 1938, the great men of one chiefdom were quarrelling. The great rain-priest, Kasitile, was ailing, and rituals were celebrated for his recovery. Godfrey Wilson watched these over three years. Kasitile sacrificed to his father; the chief to his shades. Gradually, the causes of conflict were made explicit as Kasitile, the other priests, and the chief drank beer together, and spoke out, voicing their anger,[1] and acknowledging that, in the interests of the country, they must work together.

Radcliffe-Brown argued a generation ago that the effectiveness of a ritual bore no relation to the reality of belief. He was fond of quoting Confucius in support of the view that it did not matter what a man believed so long as he celebrated aright.[2] I agree that the celebration of any ritual may modify the behaviour of the participant who is a believer. If he is not a believer – even a part-time believer, or one who reinterprets in secular form some traditionally transcendental rite – I do not think the ritual has any bite left. There must always be a connection between the symbol as it is interpreted, and reality as it is conceived, if a ritual is to modify the behaviour of the participants.

As a Christian, I go much further. I believe that God exists and that communication between God and man is fostered through participation in Christian ritual: to me it is indeed 'a means of grace'. There is more in the celebration than the participation of men. But that conclusion is based on faith not science. Furthermore, I believe that the rituals of pagan Nyakyusa and Mpondo express fundamental realities about the relations of kinsmen, and they reflect some glimmers of understanding of the nature of God. I

[1] M. Wilson, *Communal Rituals*, pp. 123-41.

[2] Radcliffe-Brown, *Structure and Function in Primitive Society* (London, 1952), p. 158.

believe that Christian rituals are a fuller expression of the nature of God and of the relations of man with man. The criterion of truth is love.

False beliefs also exist and are expressed in rituals or ceremonials, and they are dangerous to society and to individuals because of their falsehood. The criterion of falsehood is hate. I think of ceremonials, such as Nuremberg rallies, which extol hatred of groups other than the 'in-group', which defend exploitation of 'the other', which celebrate the use of force to compel conformity with what is defined as true. Attempts to compel belief through the Inquisition, through depriving people of political rights, or access to the courts, or the right to attend school and Universities, or to travel abroad, because they will not worship in the accepted form, are all expressions of false beliefs, whether the beliefs are formulated in transcendental or secular terms.

Participation in rituals by believers has effects on the community which some anthropologists and sociologists have thought so important that they question whether a society can exist without them. Durkheim implicitly accepted social cohesion – social integration – as the ultimate good; rituals made for social cohesion, and therefore rituals were good. Durkheim was expressing his own beliefs, rather than those of the Australian aborigines, when he concluded that what men worshipped was society itself.

In changing Africa traditional rituals disappear. Some disappear faster than others. Among the Xhosa I have watched initiation for girls at puberty vanish while the circumcision ritual for young men remained; and among the Nyakyusa I saw the twin ritual disappear while the death ritual continued to flourish. It is not always the same ritual which survives: circumcision disappeared among the Zulu though not among the Xhosa, and among the Ngwato but not among the Pedi. In both cases the groups are culturally similar. Xhosa ritual was tied to a pastoral economy and cannot be celebrated in traditional form in a town. Nor are the prolonged funeral rites anywhere compatible with wage labour. This used to be a matter of much concern to Nyakyusa in employment who feared an accusation of witchcraft if they failed to attend the funeral of a kinsman or neighbour. Some adjustment in social demands was made fairly rapidly, as it was at the Reformation when numerous Holy Days proved incompatible with the Puritan dogma that man's vocation was to labour. The wake is still a great social occasion in any African township in the Republic but it is timed for a week-end or public holiday; and commemoration dinners, birthday dinners, and dinners for brides regularly replace ritual killings which were traditionally obligatory.

Rituals prepared people for a change in social role, and where the society is in revolution the specific teaching becomes out of date, as when Xhosa youths are admonished to 'buy cattle' at their initiation in the Ciskei where grazing scarcely exists,[1] or a Nyakyusa Christian girl is admonished to 'cook for strangers' which she cannot do in a town; but the underlying ideas – that the circumcised man should act like an adult, not squandering his wealth but building up the homestead, and that the girl should practise the virtue of hospitality – these remain.

The problem lies not in adaptation of the content of rituals to changing circumstance but in loss of certainty as to their necessity and appropriateness. The traditional defence of a ritual among Mpondo or Nyakyusa was 'this is our custom'

[1] M. Wilson, *et al.*, *Social Structure*, Keiskammahoek Rural Survey, vol. III (Pietermaritzburg, 1952), pp. 217-19.

(*lisiko* or *lulwiho*) with the rider that if it is neglected 'we fall ill' or 'we go mad'. The difficulty is to achieve congruity and pertinence with that authority which derived from the belief that what one's fathers had done was right, and piety consisted in following precisely the customs laid down. The girls' initiation ritual among the Xhosa, or the twin ritual among the Nyakyusa is no longer felt to be relevant by most people; though Xhosa men's initiation or Nyakyusa funeral rites are felt to be relevant.

A second difficulty is that during periods of rapid social change consciousness of symbolism diminishes. I learnt this first from the poet, Kathleen Raine. She wrote of 'the forgotten language' of Blake;[1] and to those who have not enjoyed the traditional English education that was rooted in the classical studies much English poetry is obscure. When I, a barbarian from South Africa, read T. S. Eliot with the present Mistress, and other scholars, in Girton, I was floundering and wondered what he was talking about until they patiently explained to me the classical references. The 'forgotten language' keeps cropping up. Sean O'Faolain told in *The Listener* of watching an Irishman pour out on the ground the first cup from an illicit still:

'Why do you empty that cup?'
'I dunno, we always do it.'

So too, an educated Xhosa – a minister – asked me recently: 'What does the killing of an ox at a funeral *really* mean?'

The most dramatic loss of understanding I have noted was that between successive generations in BuNyakyusa. In 1938 virtually everyone had some understanding of the symbolism: by 1955 very many young men were without that understanding.

[1] Kathleen Raine, 'A Traditional Language of Symbols', *The Listener*, 9 October 1958.

The Xhosa people have long despised the Coloured community in South Africa as 'people without customs'. They, themselves, cling to a great body of traditional custom (as well as to their language) perhaps with an obscure apprehension that the loss of a man's ancient roots and symbols leaves him unable to 'ritualize his conflicts and feel at home in the world'.[1]

The new Christian community keeps feeling after an Interpreter to guide each convert, and it is no accident that the most symbolic book of the Puritan tradition has lent itself to translation into Bantu languages as none other. A magnificent Xhosa translation of *The Pilgrim's Progress*, *Uhambo Lomhambi*, by Tiyo Soga, appeared in 1866; it was proceeded by a translation into Tswana[2] and followed by translations into Bemba, Konde (a form of Nyakyusa) and many other languages in Africa.

The growing point of rituals in Africa, where the traditional and modern are welded, is in the Independent Churches. Every Independent Church lays more emphasis on ritual than the Church from which it sprang, and this process of reinterpretation and expression of Christian teaching in African idiom has been going on in the south for almost a hundred years. Drum, dance, and vestment modify the austere traditions of Protestant Europe, for the Protestant Churches were primarily concerned with instruction in beliefs and conduct: they paid scant attention to unconscious attitudes which find expression in ritual.[3]

[1] P. Mason, *Encounter*, April 1968. Cf. F. B. Welbourn, 'A Note on Types of Religious Society', C. G. Baëta (ed.), *Christianity in Tropical Africa*, p. 138.

[2] *Loeto loa Mokereseti* (Kuruman, 1848).

[3] Welbourn, 'A Note on Types of Religious Society', p. 138.

The process of indigenization is a knife edge as many African Christians, and many missionaries, are aware. Symbolism is rooted in the subconscious and some bridge from old to new is necessary if converts are to achieve any emotional depth. On the other hand many African Christians fear lest divergence from traditional Christianity will take away something from the unique Christian message, and also from the unity of Christendom.[1] The problem of translation in space and time recurs again and again: how can the gospels be interpreted intelligibly without loss of the essential message?

The anthropologist grows familiar with the idea, long proclaimed by poets, that truths first expressed symbolically are only later defined scientifically. Shakespeare showed how disharmony in the world of men was reflected in the physical elements[2] three centuries before soil scientists talked about soil erosion being a sign of bad administration; the ancient Egyptians linked a good Pharaoh with good floods; and right down through Africa to the Transkei the fertility of the fields was linked to the fertility of the chief. As Bertrand de Jouvenel has remarked, 'for perhaps tens of thousands of years men have been aware of a correspondence between the functioning of political authorities and the well-being of the group. This correspondence found expression in a language little understood by us – the mythological . . . The enrichment of life due to organization has been conceived as a boon provided by invisible powers.'[3] So too,

[1] I have benefited from discussion with the Rev. Desmond Tutu on this point.

[2] G. I. Duthie, Introduction to *King Lear* (New Shakespeare edition, Cambridge, 1960).

[3] B. de Jouvenel, *Sovereignty* (Cambridge, 1957), pp. 35, 37.

in Africa, long before Freud analysed the dreams of his Viennese patients, it was understood that dreams were an expression of conflict; before Erikson spoke of loss of identity, African villagers talked of those with majesty, authority, casting a shadow (*nesitunzi* in Xhosa), and those torn within casting no shadow.[1]

For self-understanding man requires both the intellectual formulation and the image. There is a sense of being lost both when men cease to be aware of traditional symbols and when these are no longer felt to be adequate. One of the continuing needs of any society is appropriate imagery through which men may achieve some measure of self-consciousness. The need for familiar symbols is the reality behind the truth so much exaggerated in the policy of Bantu education in South Africa: children benefit most from early education in the mother tongue, and related to their immediate environment. But in South Africa this truth has been fashioned into a strait-jacket to restrict growth. The intellectual understanding and imaginative awareness of the changing society that comes through study of the ideas and images of those of other traditions is starved.[2]

Ritual draws sanctity from antiquity, but it must be felt relevant to the celebrant's world or it becomes an empty shell. The problem in Africa, as elsewhere, is to combine sanctity with relevance in a runaway world.

[1] P. Mason, in *Encounter*, April 1968.

[2] Under the system of Bantu education African children first hear of communities outside South Africa in the seventh year of schooling. Only 0.3% of those who attend school reach this stage. J. W. MacQuarrie, *The Main Needs for the Future in African Education*, South African Institute of Race Relations Conference, January 1969 (Johannesburg).

IV. MORALITIES

In the traditional African societies with which I am familiar there is a *direct* connection between religion and morality. Such a direct link has been denied by a formidable array of scholars reflecting on anthropological material, and even by some field-workers, whose own evidence confounds them.[1] The connection can be denied, or called 'vague' or 'indirect' only if the symbolism is not understood, or 'morality' is most narrowly interpreted. Most scholars admit that right behaviour is thought to be mystically rewarded, and wrong-doing mystically punished in the societies they describe, but some still deny any close connection between religion and morality. Conceptions of right behaviour and of sin differ. Incest, murder, theft, adultery, covetousness, injury to kinsmen or neighbours, bearing false witness, failing to honour parents or care for dependants – all these are condemned, but they are variously defined. Honouring one's father among the Nyakyusa included never eating with him, or joining him at beer, or even sleeping in the same village; and avoiding incest among the Mpondo meant not marrying a girl of one's own or one's mother's clan, or that of either grandmother.

Furthermore, since the traditional religions of Africa were not monotheistic, the sources of retribution conceived of were diverse. They included the shades, the heroes,

[1] E. Tylor, *Primitive Culture* (London, 1871), 1920 edition, 2 vols, I, 427; A. Macbeath, *Experiments in Living* (London, 1952), *passim*; Junod, II, 427-8, 583; but cf. I, 80, 161-2, 323, II, 398-40; E. J. and J. D. Krige, 'The Lovedu of the Transvaal', in D. Forde (ed.), *African Worlds*, pp. 73, 80; J. Maquet, 'The Kingdom of Ruanda' in *African Worlds*, pp. 183-5.

living senior kin and village headmen, neighbours and age-mates, all of whom were thought to exercise mystical power.

The basis of morality among the Nyakyusa was the fulfilment of obligations to kinsmen, living and dead, and to neighbours, living in amity with kin and neighbours, showing respect to seniors and fulfilling obligations to dependants. Fertility was the ultimate value, and it was injured by evil-doers.[1]

The behaviour judged to be immoral was first, anger, brooding anger, unconfessed, that might drive a man to use witchcraft or sorcery; secondly, quarrelling between kinsmen which angered the shades; thirdly, disrespect to a senior kinsman, whether living or dead. Disrespect of this sort included eloping with a junior wife of one's father, own or classifactory. This was the classic sin of a society in which polygyny was approved, and men over fifty who controlled the wealth in cattle continued to marry young wives, leaving their sons in their late twenties and early thirties to live as bachelors. Accounts of such elopements recur in Nyakyusa mythology, and we recorded a number of cases which happened in the nineteen-thirties. The elopements were not only myth. A breach of the rules of avoidance by a wife was also a form of disrespect to senior kin. A woman showed respect to her husband's father and men identified with him by never looking at him and disappearing into the bush or the bananas if he were reported to be approaching. I once watched the misery of a Christian woman whose father-in-law entered the room in which we were sitting. She claimed that, as a Christian, she 'did not avoid much' but she turned

[1] Godfrey Wilson, 'An African Morality', *Africa*, **9** (1936), pp. 75-98; M. Wilson, *Rituals of Kinship*, pp. 8, 226-8; *Communal Rituals*, pp. 145-51, 160-1.

grey and sweat streamed down her face in the terror of that moment.[1]

The worst insult of all was neglect to celebrate traditional rituals, not slaughtering cows at a funeral and not offering beer to the shades. It was said: they 'are concerned that they should not be forgotten'.[2] 'They are hungry and wish to eat',[3] and as noted earlier, the form of the offering to them was closely similar to the slaughter of an animal or the brewing of beer for an honoured guest. Sacrifices and libations were their due. The occasions were death, puberty and marriage, birth, reconciliation after a quarrel between kinsmen, and at irregular times when illness or other misfortune was attributed to their hunger or dissatisfaction.[4] The expressed wish was for recovery of the patient's fertility and 'peace between us', that is, between the living and the shades. The offerings can scarcely be called worship, though they included an invocation of the shades: rather they were family feasts in which living and dead participated.

The fourth type of behaviour judged wrong was *greed.* Conspicuous success was commonly judged to be at another's expense, and therefore wrong. For example, fertility in fields was thought of as limited and the woman whose field was unusually productive was believed to have enticed away the fertility from a neighbour's land, by using medicines, or by starting to plant before her neighbour. The rule was that those whose fields adjoined must keep in step; for certain crops they must cultivate, plant, and reap together lest she who started first steal the fertility from her neighbours. In every society, competition is permitted in some

[1] M. Wilson, *Good Company* (London, 1951), pp. 84-5.
[2] Colson, p. 7.
[3] Hunter, pp. 242-50.
[4] M. Wilson, *Rituals of Kinship, passim;* Hunter, pp. 150-5, 165-74.

forms and limited in others. In the West, more especially in the United States, success in economic competition is approved and encouraged: in Africa it was not. The Nyakyusa man who grew more beans than his neighbour, or the woman who carried a heavier load of firewood resented any comment on his or her success, taking such comment as an expression of envy. I was reprimanded for expressing astonishment at the weight my neighbours could carry. It suggested I was jealous. And a Pedi man who ran a successful taxi business in Pretoria was regarded as too dangerously successful. The comment was: 'He will die soon.' He did die – eventually! But among the Nyakyusa, display by young men in a swaggering dance, or by Mpondo in miming their exploits in war, or by Pedi in singing songs about themselves and their ancestors was approved. When I heard of these songs I thought of Mr Toad of Toad Hall and how the the songs he sang about his exploits in a motor-car were the last straw. Ratty and Mole sat on him. Children's books are, of course, a rich source from which to discover the approved values of a society, or of a particular class in a society.

Greed and conspicuous wealth were thought of among the Nyakyusa as merging into the sort of greed for meat that led to witchcraft. A witch was pictured as one who gnawed the living inside until they wasted away, and who disinterred corpses to eat them. Cannibalism and witchcraft were sometimes scarcely distinguishable in ordinary speech.

I have argued that fertility was the most inclusive value of Nyakyusa society, and that fertility turned on the right use of sex. Anything thought to injure the reproductive powers of man or woman, or health of children was wrong. Hence a thicket of taboos surrounding child-birth and sexual life. A sexually active man or woman approaching an infant was thought dangerous to the infant, so a mother with a new-born baby was secluded and the midwife was extremely careful who entered the hut, or even greeted the mother from outside. The sex activities of successive generations were rigidly separate lest, in some mystical fashion, the one injure the other. A parent must not 'overstep' – or overreach – a child, or a child a parent. Thus a woman must be careful not to bear a child after her son's marriage lest that cause him to be sterile; she and her husband must live apart during the months of her daughter's initiation lest the daughter be sterile. Spacing of children was enforced, for if the mother became pregnant again within two years it was believed that the older child would suffer. Wide spacing of two to four years was explicitly for the welfare of children, and among the Nyakyusa I heard many caustic comments on the irresponsibility of European missionaries in this matter.

The adultery of a wife might kill her husband; the adultery of a husband during his wife's pregnancy might kill her or the child; the adultery of a son with one of his father's wives was not only an insult, but might kill the father. So it went on. And there were innumerable rules regarding a woman's behaviour during menstruation and pregnancy. A woman, when menstruating, might not blow up a fire lest she injure her husband who warmed himself at that fire, or injure the food cooked on it. Any contact with her, and especially her breath, was thought dangerous to him. A pregnant mother might not stand or hesitate in a doorway. She must walk straight through, lest the child hesitate also, and delivery be prolonged. In a number of contexts the hut is a symbol for the womb, and the doorway, associated with the shades, for the vagina.

A pregnant woman must not walk through a field with a sprouting crop, or approach women winnowing out grain, lest the crop be blighted or the grain diminish, for different sorts of growth – that in the fields and that in the womb – were felt to be antagonistic. The unborn child was pictured as voracious and magically snatching the grain. Nor must a pregnant woman approach a forge, for forging iron and forging a child were alike and antagonistic. And a menstruating woman might not go near cattle, lest she injure them.

From the point of view of the Nyakyusa these taboos were comparable to rules of hygiene. They were concerned with the health of parents and child, and respect for property which mother or child might injure. From the point of view of the scientist they differed from rules of hygiene because they were based, not on observation of cause and effect, but on a feeling of likeness, and things felt to be alike were taken as inextricably connected and often antagonistic. The taboos were based on magical associations unfamiliar to a European, but understandable when interpreted.

Radcliffe-Brown made much of the argument that in small societies many taboos derived from physiological conditions – birth, death, menstruation, pregnancy – and that to be born or die, or suffer menses or pregnancy was not immoral.[1] Of course not, but 'dirt' or 'infection', however defined, is not to be identified with immorality. What is immoral is failing to take proper precautions against injuring people or their property through contact with 'dirt' or 'infection' as defined in that society. The careless mother is censured everywhere. An English mother who knowingly let a child suffering from smallpox play with others would surely be condemned: so would one who knowingly offered milk infected with typhoid, or, when herself pregnant, visited a household where she knew there was German

[1] Radcliffe-Brown, p. 173.

measles. For a Nyakyusa woman who was pregnant to approach a forge and so, it was thought, destroy the metal being worked, was as immoral as it is for a Cambridge woman to allow her child to burn a friend's manuscript. The argument that observance of taboos has nothing to do with morality is only tenable if taboos are taken literally and the symbolic associations ignored. Radcliffe-Brown was guilty of that misplaced concreteness against which A.N. Whitehead warns us.

Moral rules were explicitly taught in initiation rituals, and the links between observance of taboo and morality made plain. The moral content of the Bemba girls' initiation ritual is brilliantly demonstrated by Dr Richards in her study, *Chisungu.*[1] She shows the miming of moral obligations during the ritual: miming of the proper submission of a girl to her husband, of the distribution of food to the family, and of the exchange of gifts. She shows the clay model representing 'the squat and unattractive figure of the lazy wife', and she explains how snatches of songs learnt during initiation are sung, later on, to remind a woman of her duty. The song about the mother who leaves her baby alone in the house so that it gets burnt, was sung to a young wife planning to go off to a beer drink.

It can be shown that the relationships in which conflict regularly occurs vary with the society. In a patrilineal, patrilocal society such as the Mpondo, in which a son lives in his father's homestead and takes his wife there, the commonest conflicts are between mother and daughter-in-law, between co-wives, and between wives of different brothers living in the homestead. In a matrilineal society the conflicts are between uncle and nephew or more precisely mother's

[1] Richards, *Chisungu*, pp. 120-69.

brother and sister's son, or a young man and his mother's brother's son, for authority is exercised not by the father but the mother's brother, and there is commonly friction over inheritance, a man owing obligations to his sister's son, but often favouring his own son. All this is reflected in accusations of witchcraft and sorcery, one of the expressions of friction in a society.[1]

It is observable also that the form of sin – the besetting sin – varies with the social structure. As was indicated earlier the Mpondo, who have rigid rules of exogamy which exclude marriage or love-affairs with a large number of the girls and women whom a man meets, have an elaborate theory of 'familiars', mostly fabulous animals, but also baboons and snakes, which are supposed to become the lover of master or mistress. Significantly, in contemporary South African society with its prohibition of marriage and extra-marital sex relations across the colour line, the familiar is thought often to appear as a light-coloured man or girl. The familiar is the embodiment of sexual temptation, and closely linked with dreams.[2] Furthermore, it can be shown that these ideas have spread among Sotho-speaking people who were without them, and this spread coincides with the system of migrant labour whereby husbands and wives are separated for long periods – sometimes for five years or more – the men working in towns and mines and farms, the wives remaining in the reserves with their children.[3]

Among the Nyakyusa who prohibit marriages only between immediate kin, the descendants of a common grand-

[1] M. Wilson *et al.*, *Social Structure*, pp. 170-86; M. G. Marwick, *Sorcery in its Social Setting* (Manchester, 1965), pp. 146-67, 210-58.

[2] M. Wilson, 'Witch Beliefs and Social Structure', *American Journal of Sociology*, **56**, 4 (1951), 307-13.

[3] Professor E. J. Krige, verbal communication relating to Lobedu.

father or great-grandfather, the witch is not thought to have a 'familiar' who becomes a lover, but the witch is depicted as ravenous for flesh, human flesh, if not beef. Greed for meat rather than lust for forbidden women is reflected in Nyakyusa witch beliefs. I have argued that, since the Nyakyusa live in age-villages not with kinsmen, a Nyakyusa man has less concern with preserving the cattle he sees daily passing his homestead than an Mpondo has, and grows impatient for their slaughter.[1] If a rich neighbour is stingy with feasts the witches are pictured as gnawing his entrails. I ask myself whether the concern of the medieval Church with *incubi* and *succubi*, and the increase in accusations of practising witchcraft in the seventeenth century, was not associated with rigid sex prohibitions and perhaps a change in the seventeenth century in the sex code enforced.

The moral order was thought to be maintained among the Nyakyusa first by the mystical power of senior kinsmen. As noted earlier, there was a lively belief that the just anger of a senior living kinsman – a man or woman who had authority over one, as a parent, a grandparent, a brother or sister of father, or mother's brother who had received cattle for her, one's own elder brother or sister – might injure one. The anger of all these was feared. In Nyakyusa thought they did not act alone but in concert with the shades.[2] Injured parents muttered together over the fire and the shades heard. The erring son might fall ill, or his child die, or his wife fail to conceive, or his cattle slip their calves. And if parents neglected their obligations to the shades the children suffered. For example, if a father failed to kill the bull of puberty when his daughter married, and did not offer the sacred cut at his

[1] M. Wilson, 'Witch Beliefs', pp. 311-12.
[2] M. Wilson, *Rituals of Kinship*, pp. 205-21.

shrine in the banana grove, notifying them of the marriage, the daughter might fail to conceive.[1]

Furthermore, a father's contemporaries, his neighbours in the age-village, supported him in enforcing discipline, and if his son offended him the neighbours also had to be placated and share in the feast of reconciliation.[2] Since the Nyakyusa built not with kinsmen but with age-mates, the responsibility of neighbours for enforcing moral rules was distinguished from the responsibility of kin. If neighbours were shocked or 'astonished' at the behaviour of a member of the village they murmured (the word was that used for the humming of a hive of bees) and their breath, 'the breath of men' (*embepo syabandu*), was said to fall on the sinner as a chilling fever. In short, adverse public opinion, legitimately exercised, was thought to be mystically dangerous. But its range was short: it extended only within the village in which one lived, and a man who fell ill and was aware of criticism would move to another village for that reason. So, also, a chief who had given a decision in a land dispute between two villages was careful never to sleep in the village which lost the case.

The 'breath of men' operated much like the anger of senior kinsmen, but outside the kinship network, and its source was not the shades but mystical power within men, and particularly the village headman. This power was akin to witchcraft: it was pictured by the Nyakyusa as deriving from a python in the belly, but whereas the headman and his supporters only had one python, a witch had two. That symbolism was not maintained consistently: the essential difference between the 'breath of men' and witchcraft was that the 'breath of men' was generally approved, whereas witchcraft was condemned. Those who supposed them-

[1] *Ibid.* pp. 111-12.

[2] Wilson, *Good Company*, pp. 76, 107, 156, 240.

selves victims of the 'breath', and their immediate kin, might refer to 'witchcraft', but the general opinion in the village was usually clear enough: this misfortune was due to witchcraft; that, a man had brought on himself by wrong-doing, and the 'breath' had fallen on him.

The 'breath of men' was particularly important in that it was thought to fall on those in authority who misused their power. Chiefs feared it, so did village headmen, priests and rainmakers, or the heir to a fortune who neglected his dependants – the elderly women and children inherited along with cattle.

Much less has been written about mystical power operating as a moral force outside the confines of kinship than about the power of the shades, but there is good reason to suppose that belief in a power like the 'breath of men' was widespread in Africa.[1] It was conspicuous where age-organizations were developed, and its elaboration among the Nyakyusa was linked to their form of village. They alone of the African peoples on whom we have evidence lived through life in age-villages. And so deeply rooted was the notion that the legitimate anger of neighbours and seniors brought misfortune it was carried over in the Christian community in BuNyakyusa, and I found Christian villagers, living with fellow converts, fearing the just anger of the missionary or elder, and attributing sterility to the neglect of a bridegroom to provide a feast for his neighbours at the marriage.[2]

Witchcraft and sorcery are, by definition, the misuse of mystical power; nevertheless they were thought, indirectly, to maintain the moral order, for the good man did not arouse

[1] M. Wilson, *Good Company*, pp. 167-9.

[2] Monica Hunter, 'An African Christian Morality', *Africa*, **10** (1937), 273-6.

enmity, and therefore had little to fear from witches or sorcerers. A Christian friend drew my attention to this when she remarked that it was very difficult to bring up children with good manners in the new Christian society since one was forbidden to admonish them to fear witches.[1] A pagan mother would say: 'Greet people politely that they may not be angered by you', implying 'that they may not work witchcraft against you'.

The founding heroes, as well as the immediate ancestors of particular families, were concerned with morality among the Nyakyusa. The living representatives of the heroes and commoner priests were obliged to offer sacrifices to their founders: everyone believed that the fertility and welfare of the country depended on this. Moreover, those who sacrificed must be in love and charity one with another or the sacrifice would not be efficacious. This involved cooperation and amity between independent chiefs, and between the chiefs and hereditary priests, descendants of village headmen of former generations. Quarrelling between independent chiefs, even between priests and chiefs of BuNyakyusa and those of another language group, the Kinga, who joined with the Nyakyusa in sacrifice to a common hero, Lwembe, was thought to result in drought, flood, cold weather in which the crops did not ripen, scorching heat, or epidemic disease. Quarrels within the chiefdom between a chief and his brother were cited as the cause of wild pig destroying the gardens; reconciliation as the cause of the arrival of a pride of lion which ate the pig. They were 'good lion'; they did not attack men or cattle, only pig. Wild pig are the cultivator's worst enemy in much of Africa. Other quarrels between a senior Nyakyusa priest and his fellow priests were cited

[1] M. Wilson, *Good Company*, p. 130.

as the causes of declining fertility, and inconvenient local rain which spoiled a funeral dance.[1]

The Nyakyusa belief that the fertility and welfare of the country turned on members of independent chiefdoms participating in common sacrifices, and being in love and charity one with another when they did so, was in no sense peculiar in Africa. A similar situation among the Tallensi in Ghana was magnificently described by Professor Fortes in 1936,[2] and comparable cases are reported from all over Africa. It is therefore certain that moral rules governing public life were supported by religious sanctions. But you will notice that in analysing Nyakyusa morality I have not mentioned God. I said earlier that I doubted whether God could be distinguished from the founding heroes in the traditional thought of either Nyakyusa or Mpondo. Their religion, and I think that of most peoples of south and central Africa, centred not on God, but on shades and heroes, and it was the shades and heroes who were the bulwark of morality. West Africa and the Sudan were different in this regard.

In Nyakyusa thought there was an awareness of the reality of evil. As was shown earlier (p. 36), it was conceived of as something within men – the anger, jealousy, and lust which found expression in witchcraft – but also as something extending beyond them. A terrible sin, such as incest or parricide, was widely believed to transmit power. The most potent medicines were said only to work for the man who lay with his sister, or killed his father or brother. I think that myths of incest as the origin of royal lines, and celebration

[1] M. Wilson, *Communal Rituals*, pp. 69, 117-18.

[2] Meyer Fortes, 'Ritual Festivals and Social Cohesion in the Hinterland of the Gold Coast', *American Anthropologist*, **38**, 4 (1936), 590-604.

of incest in certain royal rituals,[1] sprang from this belief. The terrible sin was felt to confer the power necessary to a ruler. Thus the myth of royal incest was the African equivalent to the myth of Faust selling his soul to the devil.

Anger was conceived as injuring those against whom it was directed whether it was justly exercised by senior kinsmen, and by neighbours or age-mates, or unjustly by witches. To avert evil the anger must be admitted. Hence, at every Nyakyusa family ritual the kinsmen who gathered to sacrifice, or the priests and chiefs who gathered for an offering to heroes, were urged to 'speak out' (*ukusosya*): to discuss their quarrels openly, to cease cherishing some grudge in secret. So at the conclusion of a funeral, or at the initiation of a girl, there was sometimes a regular slanging match, one woman telling how meanly she was received when she went to visit her brother's wife, another complaining of an unjust division of the inheritance, another of her treatment by her husband. As noted earlier, the symbol for expressing good will, thereby acknowledging that any anger which may have existed is expressed and got rid of, is to spit or blow out water.

Great stress was laid on the outward act – the blowing out of water, the eating and drinking together and the expression of good will – but the element of the inward and spiritual was not absent. It was anger *within*, unconfessed, that was dangerous and corrupting. Misfortune was linked to sin. Many of the afflictions that befell men were attributed to their own wrong-doing in neglecting their shades, or offending their kinsmen and neighbours. It is true that witches and sorcerers were thought to attack the just, but as already explained, the man who walked humbly and was generous

[1] E. J. and J. D. Krige, *The Realm of a Rain Queen* (London, 1943), pp. 5-12, 307-8.

did not readily incur envy; moreover among the Nyakyusa, at least, the just were thought to be protected against witchcraft by their village headmen and the other strong men (*abamanga*) of the village. So suffering was made endurable.

As was noted earlier, there was no idea in Nyakyusa and Mpondo tradition that an offering to the shades was a replacement. The sacrifice was a reconciliation between the living and the dead – the shades and their living kin who feasted together – but there was no hint that one man suffered for another. I think that the idea of the Suffering Servant was the creation of Israel.

We come then to the change in morality as Africa ceases to be isolated, and the Christian gospel is preached.

In the small societies of Africa, of which I have taken Nyakyusa and Mpondo as typical, the range of moral obligations was very narrow. The shades were concerned only with obligations to kinsmen; they were not concerned with behaviour towards other people. And the heroes and shades of a chief were concerned with the behaviour of great men of a chiefdom to one another, and to neighbouring chiefs if they joined in common sacrifices, but this did not stretch beyond perhaps half a million people at the most, and often no more than a fraction of that. The 'breath of men' and witchcraft were feared only from those with whom you were in immediate face-to-face relationships. In Nyakyusa thought these did not operate beyond the village, though sorcery might extend a little further. A traveller in a strange chiefdom might be speared, and the slayer was no murderer.

One of the immediately visible changes is the expansion of moral obligations as relationships extend. I heard Nyakyusa Christians admonishing a bride at her marriage: 'You are a Christian, cook for strangers. If someone dies of hunger it is your sin.'[1] And people spoke constantly about the change created by the extending rule of law which made it safe to travel among strangers. This particular change was much less apparent among the Mpondo who, three hundred years ago, already recognized a traveller as under the protection of the chief, but even among the Mpondo morality was tied to kinship and chiefdom. The radical change is in the interpretation of 'who is my neighbour?' and the acknowledgement that it includes the Samaritan, the Outsider, the man of another complexion. Some change inevitably occurs as societies expand in scale, for the recognition of some moral obligations beyond one's immediate kin is a condition of wider interaction; but there is visible all round us the conflict between extending interaction and the refusal to acknowledge the man who is different as a neighbour. Nowhere is this more apparent than in my own country.

You will note two things: first the empirical connection between the range of interaction and the range of moral obligations acknowledged; and secondly, the fact that the Samaritan was asserted to be a neighbour in a community which, though a colony of Rome, was in no sense yet part of a world society. A universal ethic was asserted and maintained by Peter and Paul, long before universal relationships existed.

Christianity escaped from the strait-jacket of kinship – 'My mother and my brethren are those which hear the word of God and do it'[2] – but the struggle between wider and narrower interpretations of moral obligations continues. In Elizabethan times in England some thought it right to put the interests of kinsmen before those of the state. In various African states this is still an acute issue. And in Europe

[1] M. Wilson, *Rituals of Kinship*, p. 201.
[2] Luke 8:21.

many people regard it as right to put the interests of their country before those of international organizations. The servant of the United Nations, whose loyalties are international, is a new breed. For a South African it is still surprising as well as encouraging to find a Calvinist theologian asserting that: 'Nationalism which extols differences and makes them sacred and exclusive values is a pernicious form of paganism.'[1]

Part of the content of morality is mutual trust, and it is apparent that any extension of the range of relations depends upon extension of trust. Trade, intellectual communication, the rule of law all depend upon a measure of mutual trust, and they break down on boundaries between states where trust has ceased to exist.

Along with the extension of the range of moral obligations there is a growth of individual freedom from immediate kin and neighbours, which we noted in Chapter I. This may involve a selfish individualism, a disregard for the needs of others. Elderly Nyakyusa talked scathingly in the 1930s of the selfishness of 'clerks who ate alone' instead of sharing their food with others as a good man should.[2] And Victor Turner has shown how an Ndembu, if he is to save money – to be thrifty and successful in terms of the modern economy – 'must break the corporate kinship nexus . . . he cannot both save and distribute money'.[3]

Is the modern western Christian more selfish than a pagan Nyakyusa or Mpondo? I suggest that good men are not, though their obligations are different. They fulfil obligations to immediate family, profession or firm, state, particular

[1] A. Biéler, *The Social Humanism of Calvin* (English translation, Richmond, Virginia, 1964), p. 21.

[2] M. Wilson, *Good Company*, p. 68.

[3] Turner, *Drums of Affliction*, p. 23.

charities, and church, rather than to extended kin and neighbours. But a man in a large society, not living in a welfare state, can be selfish if he chooses without encountering pressures as great as those which compelled a Nyakyusa, or Mpondo, or Ndembu to be generous to kinsmen. A change in the attitude towards economic competition is at least as apparent in Africa today as it was in Europe of the Reformation.

Missionaries, whether Protestant or Catholic, preaching the gospel in a pagan society, stressed the responsibility of the individual.[1] A man must choose life or death, good or evil for himself. The pagan interpretation of this was reflected in the remark of a Nyakyusa rainmaker, an elderly man whom we knew well. He said: 'If it were not for the ritual I . . . would go with my wife Jane and be baptised. If my son were old enough and had agreed to carry on the ritual I would do it . . . I would like to go and be baptised . . . But I fear for the ritual, I fear hunger, the hunger of the people. For I am the food of the country, I am the maker of food.'[2]

Whether or not responsibility for the ritual was the main reason for his rejection of Christianity he was intensely conscious of his obligations to his community. Missionaries stressed the need of 'initiative' and self-improvement. They preached a gospel of work. John Wesley wrote: 'The Methodists in every place grow diligent and frugal, and consequently they increase in goods.'[3] And the same might have

[1] Some modern missionaries are stressing family and community; cf. J. Mbiti, 'Ways and Means of Communicating the Gospel', in Baëta (ed.), p. 338: 'Evangelization of the home and household should take first priority to which "personal evangelism" can be added later.'

[2] M. Wilson, *Communal Rituals*, p. 141.

[3] Quoted by Max Weber, *The Protestant Ethic and The Spirit of Capitalism*, translated by Talcott Parsons (London, 1967, paperback), p. 175.

been said of communities on innumerable mission stations in Africa. If converts did not grow 'diligent and frugal' outsiders commonly thought the mission had failed. The stress on the gospel of work varied somewhat with the denomination or missionary society, but the view that 'Christianity and idleness are not compatible' was widespread.[1] This view is particularly apparent at the present time among Jehovah's Witnesses in Zambia.[2] It is expressed most cogently in secular terms, by Dr Nyerere in Tanzania. The Arusha Declaration, a national plan for improving community living through hard work and self-denial, is a radical development and fulfilment of earlier missionary programmes for social uplift. Dr Nyerere, himself a Christian, is trying to mould the institutions of an expanding society in terms of Christian values.

The growth of individual responsibility and independence reacts on family organization, and throughout south and central Africa there is apparent a slackening of economic obligations to more distant kin and a tendency for the elementary family to operate as a more independent economic unit than previously. It has been argued that in Britain industrialization did not cause the growth of small independent families, but the small independent family which already existed facilitated industrialization.[3] However that may be, there can be no doubt that Mpondo family units have grown smaller, and have greater economic independence, as the shift from a pastoral to an industrial society proceeds.

Other radical changes in family organization are going on.

[1] James Stewart, Paper read at the General Missionary Conference, London, 22 Oct. 1878, in *African Papers* (ed. J. Stewart).

[2] Baëta (ed.), pp. 401-3.

[3] Peter Laslett, *The World We have Lost* (London, 1965), pp. 89-96.

Traditionally among Nyakyusa and Mpondo marriages, at any rate the first marriage of a man and a girl, were the concern of their families at least as much as that of the groom and bride. Arranged marriages were approved.

There was a fundamental cleavage between Nyakyusa or Mpondo, who regarded it as proper that a girl should submit to her parents' choice of a husband for her, and that a widow should accept her late husband's heir, and white missionaries or administrators who condemned 'forced marriages'. In 1883 a Xhosa giving evidence before a Government Commission insisted that 'a thing called love' was destroying parental control and causing illegitimacy,[1] and in the 1930s the Nyakyusa generally attributed the rising divorce and illegitimacy rates to European insistence that a woman should not be compelled to marry against her will.[2] Few missionaries or administrators seemed to realize how recent freedom of choice was in Britain.[3]

The idea that a woman should be free to choose her husband and a man his wife encourages the shift from an ideal of polygyny to one of monogamy. The practice of polygyny is closely linked to particular economic conditions; notably subsistence herding or cultivation, with ample land. It diminishes or disappears when land becomes scarce, and in an industrialized society. It is also closely linked to particular demographic conditions, when marriageable women outnumber marriageable men. This may be due to a differential survival rate of men and women such as occurred in Western Europe in the 1914–18 war, and in Russia in the

[1] *Report . . . of the Government Commission on Native Laws and Customs*, G.4.-83 (Cape Town, 1883), I, 304.

[2] M. Wilson, *Communal Rituals*, pp. 207-8, 220.

[3] C. S. Lewis, *The Allegory of Love* (Oxford, 1936), *passim*. G. C. Moore Smith, *The Letters of Dorothy Osborne to William Temple* (Oxford, 1928), Letters 53, 55, 56, 75, 76.

last war; but much more often it has been due to a difference in the marriage age, so that girls of sixteen to twenty-six were married whereas men of that age were not. The demographer, Sonnabend, showed more than thirty years ago that seven years' difference in the marriage age allows twenty per cent of the men to have more than one wife.[1] Acute social difficulties occur if polygyny diminishes rapidly, whether for economic or religious reasons, and a marked difference in the marriage age of men and women or in their survival rate, remains. In South Africa, the widespread concubinage and illegitimacy rates of over fifty per cent of births among Africans are partly due to a continuing difference in the marriage age between men and women, and a probable difference in survival rate. Missionaries rarely grasped the demographic problem when they pressed for monogamy, but it is perhaps significant that it was in Zululand, where the devastating wars of Shaka and his successors had left the sex ratio markedly disturbed, that a missionary, Bishop Colenso, pressed the case for baptizing polygynists. Still, in Africa, there is deep disquiet over Church rules regarding polygyny and particularly over the rule to be applied when a polygynist seeks baptism, but it is very generally agreed that polygyny is no ideal for Christian family relationships.[2]

Polygyny implies a relatively subordinate position of women in society, and it is questioned, at least by women, when social inequalities in general begin to be questioned. Africa will hardly remain insulated from the questioning of *all* inequality which is so apparent in Europe and America.

[1] H. Sonnabend, 'Demographic Samples in the Study of Backward and Primitive Populations', *South African Journal of Economics*, **2** (1934), 319-21.

[2] Baëta (ed.), pp. 17, 141, 172-4, 220-1, 240-4, 274-5.

One of the marks of increase of scale is an extension of the range of the rule of law: the size of the group within which law is effective has expanded enormously even since the seventeenth century. But as populations increase and become more dense, problems of government increase. It is more difficult to maintain order in a great city, than in scattered villages. Lorentz has even suggested that density may create insoluble problems of aggression. Furthermore, when inequality that exists is not accepted the whole authority of government begins to crumble. I look at the present murder rate for South Africa – 21 per 100,000 a year[1] – and see how people fear to move about cities at night, and compare that with the security in a traditional chiefdom of the Transkei in 1801 when a military officer, Colonel Collins, commented that the Xhosa chief, Hintsa, maintained 'perfect security of life and property without ever condemning any person to death'.[2]

In Africa, among the people of whom I have been speaking, there was a lively awareness that moral obligations extended in time as well as space. The living acknowledge a responsibility both for the dead and for generations yet unborn. In the contemporary Western world responsibility for education of the next generation is fully accepted, and specialists in given fields are often insistent on the obligation not to squander resources such as soil, or oil; and the danger of laying waste continents by using atomic bombs,

[1] Murders for the period 1 July 1966 to 30 June 1967 were 4,161; *Annual Reports of the Commissioner of the South African Police*, R.P. 40/1968: Population of the Republic, June 1967: 18,733,000; *Bureau of Census and Statistics*, Pretoria. The South African rate is the fourth highest in the world. Compare U.S. 4·5 and England and Wales 0·6; Wolfgang and Ferracuti, *The Sub-Culture of Violence* (London, 1967), pp. 274-5.

[2] Moodie, *The Record*, v, 44.

neglecting contamination caused by men and engines, or allowing population to expand far beyond resources is acknowledged in theory. But part of the unrestrained individualism which has been so evident in Europe and America during the past century, and is now evident sometimes in Africa, is a disregard of obligations to succeeding generations. This may result in farmers 'mining the land', paying no regard to loss of fertility and soil, or townsmen neglecting the disposal of refuse and gasses.

Furthermore, obligations to past generations are admitted reluctantly. Perhaps because I am old, I see this as one of the disorders of our time. I think that recognition and acceptance of one's roots is as necessary to a group as it is to an individual. Obligations to past generations are fulfilled by acknowledging continuity and dependence, though admitting change. Any large society changes fast – and change does not necessarily involve a break in continuity – England's great success in maintaining continuity is one of her glories. But we ordinary mortals grow a bit giddy when we shift from foot safari or ox-waggon to jet plane, as my generation has done in Africa.

To conclude, in the traditional societies of Africa there was a direct connection between religion and morality, though the concepts of sin varied and the sources of retribution were diverse. They included the mystical power of senior kinsmen and 'the breath of men'. The basis of morality was fulfilment of obligation to kinsmen and neighbours, and living in amity with them. Anger in the heart was the root of evil and to avert evil anger must be admitted. As isolation diminishes the range of moral obligations extends in space and time, there is a growth of individual freedom and responsibility, and a change in family organization. The range of law extends but the difficulty of maintaining order is greater in cities than in small isolated communities.

Finally, the effect of increase in scale is an enormous increase in choice facing each individual, and any choice involves morality.

V. IMPLICATIONS FOR CONTEMPORARY SOCIETY: BELIEF AND ORGANIZATION

It was argued in the first chapter that every society has ultimate beliefs and values. Man cannot exist without them. If it is thought that reality is confined to what one can touch, see, measure, or produce by experiment, then values and morality are linked to that materialist view. Choices are determined ultimately by the view of reality one holds. The Marxists who assert 'History will absolve me' as Castro does,[1] make assumptions about the dialectic of history. They believe their assumptions to be supported by observation, but they go beyond observation, just as the Christian goes beyond observation when he asserts that love is ultimately more powerful than hate. A secular view of reality dominates much of the world, and though the idol of nationalism has been reduced in stature in Western Europe, it is re-erected in Africa and Asia, and determines policy.

Anthropologists have recognized readily enough that both transcendental religion and secular ideology make for the coherence of society. Such recognition drove Durkheim to assert that society was the object of worship everywhere, even among the Australian aborigines. It drove Radcliffe-Brown to the view that ritual was a social necessity, but it did not matter whether what was expressed in the ritual were true or false.[2]

The ultimate value for both Durkheim and Radcliffe-Brown was *social coherence*. This was never made explicit, but throughout their writings it is implied that what makes for social integration is necessarily good. Now the coherence

[1] Fidel Castro, *History Will Absolve Me* (London, 1968).

[2] Radcliffe-Brown, pp. 158-61.

of a particular society is not accepted as the ultimate good by those who seek to change it.[1] They value other things more highly than social coherence, perhaps what they conceive of as freedom, egality, brotherhood, and indeed Christian missionaries in Africa have repeatedly sought to destroy an ancient tribal cohesion.

What the Christian asks about religion is not: 'Is it useful?', 'Does it make for social coherence?', but 'Is it true?' or more accurately 'What insights into truth are there?'. No demonstration of the nature of reality, comparable to demonstration in the experimental sciences, is of course possible. I work on the hypothesis that the life, death, and resurrection of Jesus reported in the gospels are true, and that love is the ultimate power. This is faith. And starting from that premise I ask myself what are the implications in contemporary society which I, as an anthropologist, see.

Both as an anthropologist and as a Christian I see the family of parents and children as the basic unit in society without which social life cannot exist. It is there that love and trust are first learnt. But the form of the family varies enormously, and it is on form that argument turns. To me the foundation of sexual morality is care for the partner and for children, and the greatest evil is to bring unwanted children into the world. All the evidence from the observation of primates – both animals and men – indicates that the welfare of a child depends first on its early relationship with the mother. An unwanted child can rarely have the unstinted love and care that may be expected for one that is desired.

[1] Some anthropologists now question whether the concept of social coherence has any practical use. If no coherence existed there would be no society. In everyday life we take for granted regularities – rules and customs which are observed. Cf. M. Gluckman, 'The Utility of the Equilibrium Model in the Study of Social Change,' *American Anthropologist*, **70**, 2 (1968), 219-37.

Secondly, the well-being of the child depends upon adaptation in a peer group: it cannot achieve maturity – particularly emotional maturity – without friends. And the child that is brought up by parents alone – or worse still, by one parent – suffers as much as the child deprived of love and care, for demands are made upon it which it cannot meet. Nyakyusa ritual is full of symbols of over-shadowing, for it is believed that one of the worst things that can happen to a man is to be 'brooded over' by his shades as a hen broods over chickens. Some trees cast a shade under which nothing grows: others provide shelter for their own saplings and other sorts of plants without stunting them. Men are like trees in this regard.

So a balance must be struck between the home and the peer group for *both* are essential. I note that, on the one hand, those kibbutzim which brought up children communally from infancy are tending to permit more and more time with the parents, and on the other, that the isolation of a middle-class Victorian nursery is a thing of the past. It was a *local* phenomenon flourishing neither in slums nor in villages in England, nor in the English-speaking communities in America, Australia, or Africa. But we have not yet achieved forms of organization which both provide for young children and allow the mother of a young family adequate time off.

The form of the family is radically affected by demographic changes – the near doubling of expectation of life and a fall in the birth rate – and economic changes when it ceases to be the centre of economic production.[1] It also has been modified by specifically Christian values. In Africa this has

[1] Laslett, pp. 1-21.

been apparent during the past hundred years. The shift from polygyny to monogamy, the right of a widow to reject a leviratic marriage, and the right of a son or daughter to reject a distasteful marriage arranged by parents, have been pressed by Christian missions, though such changes seemed shocking to many pagans.[1]

The gospel is revolutionary, and Christianity has been a force compelling change in society for nearly two thousand years. No student of the Acts and Epistles, or of the spread of the Church – I mean here the people of God – particularly in the first centuries A.D. and the last two, can doubt this. The function of the Church is to lead, to initiate new services, new institutions, whether for the education of children and adults, or the care of the sick, the aged, the destitute, or the fostering of skills and organizing the hungry that they may feed themselves. This function was evident throughout medieval Europe:[2] it is clear in contemporary Africa.

Once the services started by the Church are accepted by a community as *necessary* then they can be, and commonly are, taken over by the state. They become 'public services' supported from taxation, and the Church can and does gradually relinquish them. Of course there is debate over the timing of the changes, and over particular services: should the Church retain this school or that hospital? Has it not still a function in setting standards or in experimenting in education? The crux is that once the Christians in a community have persuaded their fellow citizens that certain services are essential – whether education, or care of the sick and the destitute – then the time has come to turn to something new: to lead again, and to experiment. As Arch-

[1] M. Wilson, *Communal Rituals*, pp. 198-200.

[2] Herbert Butterfield, *Christianity in European History* (London, 1951) pp. 19-21.

bishop Temple said, 'The Church should not be a fortress but an expeditionary force'.

Looking at the history of southern Africa during the past two centuries, it is plain that missions played a major role in creating the shift from isolated tribal society to peasant community, no longer isolated, but trading and communicating with the outside world.[1] Each tiny mission station from Genadendal onwards[2] was a nucleus of men no longer content to live as tribesmen. They were beginning to hear of the outside world, learning to read a gospel, learning a second language, being taught new skills, given new crops and tools, seeking the goods of civilization. They became a 'people of the book', for one of the first tasks of missionaries in Africa was to write the languages of preliterate people and translate the Bible.[3]

In Europe, in Africa, and in South America the Church has been shaped by the peasant communities which it played so great a part in creating. The medieval Church flourished in a world in which peasants formed the great bulk of the population and in which it was assumed that a peasantry would always be the greater part of any society. But peasantries are not permanent,[4] and the period of their existence in southern Africa is likely to be much shorter than in Europe. Already there is evidence of growing impoverishment of peasants, partly due to population pressure, and the signs indicate a trend to large-scale mechanized farming

[1] Robert Redfield, *The Little Community* (Chicago, 1955).

[2] The first mission station in South Africa, founded by Moravians in 1738. It had a profound influence on the pattern of life and work in later missions of other communions. Krüger, *The Pear Tree Blossoms.*

[3] Wilson and Thompson (eds), II, Chapter II. Robert Redfield, *The Folk Culture of Yucatan* (Chicago, 1941); *A Village that Chose Progress* (Chicago, 1950).

[4] Bertrand Russell, *The Impact of Science on Society* (London, 1952), pp. 44-5.

and industry.[1] The Church in southern Africa, as in Europe, must adapt itself to an industrialized society.[2]

Many people try to use the Church to *prevent* change. The identification, typical of small societies, of piety with conservatism keeps reappearing. At a church conference in South Africa I once heard a Member of Parliament (an Afrikaner) assure the conference that it was immoral for Africans to abandon traditional custom, and immoral for missionaries to teach them to do so. When asked whether it was immoral for a pagan to become a Christian he was disconcerted.

Nostalgia for the village[3] – mourning for the pit-village, or any other close-knit group – recurs continually, and old ladies like myself are likely to think that the customs of our youth were more moral than the customs of students today – more moral, note, not just different. (We did not quite go to lectures with a chaperone as our seniors had done, but we were required to wear *hats*, and must now remind ourselves that hats – or skirts – are no badge of morality!)

It has been argued that the most general change occuring in society is the increase in scale, that is in the number of people interacting, and the closeness of their interaction. And with the increase in scale goes increase in knowledge and skill and therefore in power to shape society. As I said earlier, Christians cannot reject increase in scale: they have in fact continually fostered it by preaching the gospel. Tillich[4]

[1] Wilson and Thompson (eds.), II.

[2] J. V. Taylor and D. A. Lehmann, *Christians of the Copperbelt*, *passim*.

[3] Cf. G. C. Homans, *The Human Group* (London, 1951), pp. 367-8. Nostalgia for the village is evident in much of the literature of South Africa, cf. Wilson and Thompson, II.

[4] P. Tillich, *Love, Power and Justice* (New York, 1960), p. 25.

the theologian defines love as 'the drive towards the unity of the separated', and an anthropologist, Margaret Mead,[1] has argued that it is increase in scale which has given men opportunity for showing love to all the world: it is only this generation which has had the wealth and skill to treat all the world as neighbours. Some readers will remember that it was an African Christian, the great St Augustine of Hippo, who taught in the fifth century that the process of history was a process making for Christ's kingdom.

At two periods within the last two hundred years men have looked back nostalgically to small-scale societies: Rousseau wrote of 'the noble savage', and some today seem to seek an anarchy – an absence of organization – which would take us back to a small-scale existence. Those who praise small-scale societies have rarely lived in them, in isolation, for long. We anthropologists have. Those who hanker after a primitive life have not understood the implications – a world without books; a world of much sickness without effective medicine; a world without transport in which famine threatens, for where there is isolation, bad weather spells starvation;[2] a world of sameness, since hunter or cultivator, enclosed in his own tiny community, does not savour that variety which entrances the outsider visiting one isolated society and then another. I once listened to the same

[1] Margaret Mead, 'Cultural Man' in *Man in Community*, ed. E. de Vries (New York, 1966), pp. 197-235. The spoken address emphasized the point further than the published version.

[2] Cf. Thomas Hardy, *The Mayor of Casterbridge* (London, 1895, pocket edition 1906), p. 220: 'The time was in the years immediately before foreign competition had revolutionized the trade in grain, when still, as from the earliest ages, the wheat quotations from month to month depended entirely upon the home harvest. A bad harvest, or the prospect of one, would double the price of corn in a few weeks; and the promise of a good yield would lower it as rapidly.' Wilson and Thompson (eds), I, 254.

drum rhythms going continuously, night and day, for a week, at a funeral in the Nyakyusa village in which I lived, and ached for variation.

The outsider may suppose that there is a level of love and charity far surpassing that of the civilized world and overlook the fact that obligations to kin, or to feed starving neighbours are enforced by sanctions as binding as those enforcing the payment of taxes in a welfare state. Both sorts of obligation may be fulfilled with goodwill or extreme reluctance.

When opportunity to escape isolation, to establish wider contact occurs, most (though not quite all) people grasp it. Even the very isolated hunters living in the Kalahari say that once a man has moved out to live for a time as a herdsman on a farm, he cannot return to the desert.

As so often, we seek to have our cake and eat it: to enjoy some of the goods of civilization and escape the evils. It is the business of the anthropologist to show the Peter Pans who refuse to grow up, who reject the responsibilities of largeness of scale, what tiny societies are like; to show yet again, that the 'noble savage' in Arcadia is dream, not reality. To seek a return to smallness of scale is no cure for for our present disorders; rather we must examine very closely what aspects of scale necessarily hang together. Can one have the close-knit warmth and emotional security of an isolated village without stifling individuality? Can one enjoy the fruits of science and industrial production without smothering the personal?

Man finds security in belonging to a group; he escapes loneliness when he feels that he is loved and understood: 'all the genuine deep delight of life is in showing people the mud-pies you have made; and life is at its best when we confidingly recommend our mud-pies to each other's sympathetic consideration'.[1] This the man of a small-scale society may achieve among his kinsmen and neighbours. Equally, he may quarrel with them and, unable to escape them, live under a cloud, accused of practising witchcraft or fearing the witchcraft of others. In a large society a man finds friends among those with like interests. He has a much wider choice of friends than the man from a small-scale society who is bound by kinship ties, confined in space. This very choice may destroy him, as I shall try to show you, and he may live in fearful isolation. But potentially, in his marriage, in his work, in his leisure, he may achieve a sense of belonging and a level of communication which I believe far transcends that of the Nyakyusa villagers I knew. Here I am making a judgement of value: you know the premises from which I start.

In a large civilized society which is the heir of countless civilizations in the past, the heir of a multitude of artists, scholars, and saints, the heir of Christian revelation, there are greater heights and depths than in an isolated, preliterate society. I believe that the evil can be greater for self-consciousness, self-awareness has grown, but the achievements of mind and spirit can also be much greater. Again this is a judgement of value, not something that I can demonstrate experimentally.

One of the changes that occurs with increase in scale is a change in the forms and degree of social stratification. Inequality in human societies grows and diminishes in a curve different from that of the increase in scale. Small hunting groups are egalitarian, pastoralists and cultivators considerably less so, as they grow more wealthy and some

[1] J. M. Thorburn, quoted by Susanne Langer, *Philosophy in a New Key* (Cambridge, Mass., 1942), pp. lx-x.

men control either breeding stock or land which is scarce, but the highly organized industrial societies become more egalitarian again. Mr Philip Mason has argued that for a long period increasing stratification implied increasingly efficient organization, but that as a means of organization inequality is now inefficient; and industrialized society depends on invention, inspiration, and individual insight.[1] For a great part of history people acquiesced in inequality: now there is growing resentment at it. The questioning has Christian roots. It was St Paul who first preached that in Christ there is neither bond nor free, male nor female.[2] The implications of that assertion are still working themselves out in a fashion that might astonish St Paul himself, since he still assumed the existence of slavery and the subjection of women in everyday life. In Africa, as elsewhere, impatience with inequality embraces generations and sexes, as well as races, castes, and hereditary classes.

What is clear is that the existence of hierarchy is challenged today whether it is based on birth (including race) or sex, age, wealth, or education. It is not merely the office holders who are challenged by others seeking to replace them, but the very existence of any hierarchy – of foremen, or managers, or owners; of professors, bishops, or generals. The argument usually collapses with the generals and the need for some sort of authority to achieve agreed ends is admitted. Skill and knowledge are suggested as the most respectable base for authority – at least by intellectuals.

The morality of extreme differences in wealth within one nation, and particularly of poverty in the midst of plenty

[1] P. Mason, 'Human Rights and Race Relations' (unpublished lecture). I am indebted to Mr Mason for this line of thought, and for a stimulating correspondence.

[2] 1 Corinthians 12:13; Galatians 3:28.

such as exists in a number of countries, and between the rich nations and poor nations, is everywhere questioned. Increasing differences are felt to be intolerable. Christian criticism of the 'acquisitive society', and of the distribution of wealth, has been less forthright than that by Communists, but the drive to a juster economic order had Christian roots.[1] You may remember that John MacMurray spoke of Communism as a heresy of Christianity which exaggerated, as a heresy does, one aspect of the Christian message.

Britain has been in the lead in such questioning, and her achievement in raising the incomes of the poorest and providing for the young, the old, and the unfit is enormously impressive to a citizen of a country in which the poor are so hungry and the distribution of wealth is so glaringly unequal as my own. Perhaps it takes an outsider to realize how much Britain has achieved – I think particularly of the comments of Mr Chadhuri, an Indian.[2]

Resistance to increase in scale comes chiefly from those who wield power in the existing order and fear to lose it. The resistance is apparent in the maintenance of caste and class barriers in India, South Africa, and the American South. A struggle is going on in South Africa over the relation between Christianity and racial barriers. Will the Church disrupt caste[3] or help to maintain it? Conventional and legal pressures towards separate worship and separate religious organizations for those of different race are strong:

[1] Barbara Ward, *The Rich Nations and the Poor Nations* (London, 1962); *A New History* (Cape Town, 1969); John MacMurray, *The Clue to History* (London, 1938), pp. 19-20, 206-7.

[2] N. C. Chadhuri, *A Passage to England* (London, 1959), pp. 199-206.

[3] The identification of colour groups as castes is not accepted by all anthropologists but is used here in the sense in which it was used by J. Dollard, *Caste and Class in a Southern Town* (New York, 1937).

but the Catholic tradition towards the unity of believers is also strong and finds expression in such organizations as the Christian Institute led by Mr Beyers Naudé, an Afrikaner, and a former moderator of the Dutch Reformed Church in the Transvaal. A non-racial religion is inevitably a threat to a racial state and the struggle is a desperate one.

The Church in Africa tends to be identified with privilege, and above all with the whites. One of the leading South African writers, a black African, spoke of the 'Christian faith' as 'the very expression of dishonesty of the West'. But identification with privilege goes beyond the colour line. In South Africa there was an early cleavage between 'school people' who accepted mission teaching and pagans who rejected it. The depth of the cleavage was linked to the frontier wars – a hundred years of war.[1] Those who accepted Christianity and education (the two went hand in hand) became the new elite; a handful became professional men and women, many got slightly better-paid jobs in industry and commerce than did the illiterate; and the process was cumulative, for those who first secured education made great efforts to educate their children. Inevitably Christians became leaders in the new African communities; the 'school people' pursued middle-class ideals. This is one reason why in African townships, rioters commonly burn churches: the town toughs – *skollies* as we call them – are in direct opposition to those they derogatorily call 'ooscuse me', and those who call themselves 'decent people'.[2]

A reaction to colour bar within the Church began last century in the 1880s, with the establishment of an Independent African Church. It was quickly followed by others. The initial conflicts all turned on race, but soon the Inde-

[1] Wilson and Thompson (eds), I, 265; II, chapter II.
[2] Wilson and Mafeje, p. 102.

pendent Churches themselves began to split, showing conclusively that race was not the sole issue.

The followers of some, though not all, of the Independent Churches were the less educated, and it is the Independent Zionist and Apostolic Churches which attract most converts from the pagan community. Most of the older mission Churches have become middle or upper class in terms of the structure of the African community, though not in terms of South African society as a whole. In some measure it is true that the groups which continue to hive off from larger Churches are the less privileged, the dispossessed. In 1960 there were reported to be over 2,400 Independent Churches within the Republic of South Africa, with a total membership of over two million, a fifth of the African Christians.[1]

We anthropologists do not know very much yet about the reasons for coherence and splitting of groups. We can define, and even predict in certain situations, the lines of cleavage; we can trace immediate causes; and we have some notion of the critical size of different sorts of groups in different situations – lineages among the Nuer, chiefdoms among the Nguni or Sotho, rugby football clubs in Langa[2] – but we have not explained why in sixteenth-century Europe,[3] on the nineteenth-century American frontier,[4] and twentieth-century Africa there was such a rapid multiplication of little local groups. Why such rapid multiplication in these periods and not in others? All I can show you is that secular groups, such as rugby clubs, split and multiply in the same sort of way as churches in South Africa. The conditions

[1] M. Horrell, *A Survey of Race Relations in South Africa*, 1966 (Johannesburg, 1967), p. 26.

[2] Wilson and Mafeje, pp. 114-17, 175-80.

[3] Joachim Wach, *The Sociology of Religion* (Chicago, 1944), p. 191.

[4] H. Richard Niebuhr, *The Social Sources of Denominationalism* (1929, paperback, Cleveland, 1957), pp. 139-99.

determining coherence and splitting in society are perhaps the fundamental problem of social anthropology.

There is a continual tension between organization and spiritual content. Each time a group breaks away from the Church it seeks spiritual renewal and a sloughing off of dead forms, but as the first generation passes the group is faced with the problems of continuity – teaching its children, training its leaders – and of interaction with others. Either the new Church remains small and isolated or some structure linking local groups emerges. Organization cannot be avoided. One can observe this at every stage in the Independent Churches in Africa. Some Christians talk of religious organization withering. I think they are as mistaken as Karl Marx was in his prediction that the state would wither.

The process of conversion to Christianity in Africa has been through groups of friends or kinsmen in village and school. The first converts were sometimes men of substance who brought their children and dependants with them, or sons of leading families who came to learn from the strangers; they were also refugees, often ex-slaves, cared for by the missionaries, and personal followers of missionaries. But many more men and women were brought into the Church through their friends, and above all by the Church 'elders' or catechists who, within a generation of mission activity, spread through the villages.[1] Sometimes they were employed by the mission as teachers or preachers, often the elder was

[1] The evidence lies in innumerable mission reports and missionary journals. For brief summaries see: J. K. Bokwe, *Ntsikana* (Lovedale, (1914), *passim*; Krüger, pp. 21, 52; R. Oliver, *The Missionary Factor in East Africa* (London, 1952), pp. 13-26, 50-4, 60-1, 63-5; Baëta, (ed.), pp. 72-3; M. Wilson, *Communal Rituals*, pp. 166-7. For portraits of two remarkable elders see: M. Wilson, *Good Company*, plate VI; M. Wilson, *Communal Rituals*, plate 13.

the first or most active Christian in a village who conducted daily prayers and gathered followers around him. The effective agents in spreading Christianity were these tiny cells of Christians, each with its acknowledged leader, who led them in worship and study of the gospels, and who instructed would-be followers in the catechism, and in reading, that they might read the gospels for themselves.

The small band of believers, gathering for worship and fellowship, is the primary group within the Church, but in modern Africa, as in the Mediterranean world of the first century, most of them have been linked by a central organization – a Church or missionary society – which sent out teachers, found funds to support them, provided translations of the Bible, and maintained a body of doctrine which assured coherence with like believers in time and space.

Many – perhaps most – of the Independent Churches reflect a preoccupation with health.[1] It will be recalled that the rituals of traditional religions which we examined were primarily concerned with health and fertility, and the service constantly sought from missionaries in Africa has been aid for the sick. All the early missionaries provided some sort of medical aid whether they were medically qualified or not, but very soon the Churches were hastening to provide hospitals, and medical training for nurses, and later for doctors. This has been one of their major contributions. But medical work became so specialized that the ordinary priest or minister ceased to take much share in service for the sick, and in most mission congregations healing and worship became quite separate. Specialization has wrought the miracles of modern medicine, but I ask myself whether a closer link between healing and worship should not again

[1] V. E. W. Hayward (ed.), *African Independent Church Movements* (London, 1963), pp. 47-52.

be sought by Christians. If indeed the incidence and course of disease is profoundly modified by mental attitudes, must we not rethink the relationship? This is only one example of the perennial problem of how to enjoy the fruits of specialization and still connect between specialisms.

I said that the Church tended to be identified with the *status quo* and one pressing problem for Christians in Africa, and particularly also in South America, is what part they should play in changing society. If government is unjust what pressures do Christians use? For my part I exclude the use of violence – armed force – and that leaves only persuasion – a long, slow process of education. But not all the contributors to that remarkable book, *Responsible Government in a Revolutionary Age*, edited by the late Z. K. Matthews, exclude the use of force by Christians in seeking to restrain force exercised by certain governments. Some leading Christians in South America teach that there is an obligation to participate in revolution by force.[1] Violence has been defined as the destructive imposition of power, and argument turns on how best to control such violence.

We have seen that one of the manifestations of increase in scale is the growth of specialization. This implies a separation, in larger societies, between sacred and profane (or natural and supernatural) which is absent in the smaller societies. You will remember that Durkheim pinned his argument to the distinction, but that one field-worker after another in small preliterate communities has reported that no such distinction was apparent among *his* people,[2] though

[1] Z. K. Matthews (ed.), *Responsible Government in a Revolutionary Age* (New York, 1966), p. 168.

[2] Evans-Pritchard, *Witchcraft*, pp. 80-3; Lienhardt, p. 28.

he might use it as a tool for analysing evidence. There is more separation between religious ritual and secular activity in the large society than in the small, and greater separation of functions, the specialist priest being typical of the large society, while the father or chief who sacrifices on behalf of his dependants is of the small. The Church, in one aspect, is a specialist organization for worship and instruction, served by specialist priests. Many today are conscious of the danger of organizations swallowing men, and of undue specialization. We are aware of this in universities as well as in Church. The danger of tyranny by officials – the management, the administration – is implicit in increase of scale.[1] But in any large society some sort of organization is unavoidable. It is apparent when one travels in Africa or India that the organization achieved in the West is as important as its science and technology in creating a large-scale society. Poor countries want it desperately, and they gain experience of it partly through the Church. It is no accident that leaders in politics and trade unions in Africa have been drawn from the Churches. Experience in organization beyond the bounds of kinship was gained by holding office in presbytery, diocese, or circuit.[2]

There must be organization in a large society, even organization of worship and teaching. Loving God with one's mind includes efficiency in the society in which one lives. And a highly specialized society requires specialists to lead others in worship, and to teach. The priest is the leader in ritual which, I shall try to show in the next chapter, is a continuing necessity: equally we look for leadership in

[1] Russell, pp. 49-50.

[2] A. L. Epstein, *Politics in an Urban African Community* (Manchester, 1958), pp. 67, 134; Wilson and Mafeje, pp. 99-100, 179; E. P. Thompson, *The Making of the English Working Class* (London, 1963), p. 37.

thinking and teaching about God. But organization is made for man, not man for organization. As a lay person not trained in theology, it seems to me that there has been confusion between 'the Church', used to mean the community of faithful people living and dead, and 'the Church' used to mean an organization. The respect and sanctity due to the community is sometimes claimed for the organization. The organization in a diverse society never embraces everyone; it is 'a gathered Church', and this is familiar enough in countries where Christians have never formed more than a minority; but in Britain, and in Europe generally, the idea that 'the Church' should embrace the whole community and is distinguished from 'denomination' or 'sect', which represents a minority, is still strong.[1] I think it is a view which is no longer tenable. We do not live in a Christian society, but in a diverse society in which some people – larger or smaller sections of the whole – are believers. And our function as believers was defined as yeast to leaven the whole, or as salt to give it savour.[2]

The form of organization changes with the structure of society. The establishment of Churches in Africa created worshipping groups no longer based solely on kinship and locality, and as kinship and locality grow relatively less important as the basis of cooperation, so worshipping groups centred not on a parish, but on a factory or firm or profession, or other common interest, may grow. This is nothing revolutionary to those bred in the tradition of school and college chapels. A more radical change is the acknowledgement that there can be no monolithic Church coterminous with the known world. The large society is

[1] A. R. Vidler, 'Religion and the National Church', *Soundings* (Cambridge, 1962), pp. 241-63.

[2] Matthew 5:13.

diverse, and that diversity extends to belief and organization.

Furthermore, diversity is not merely accepted; often it is positively valued. 'Intolerance' is condemned. The most marked change between the medieval and modern world which I, as an anthropologist, see is the growth of toleration regarding belief about God; the acceptance that those whose transcendental beliefs differ from one's own should not be compelled to conform. Persecution in the name of God shocks this generation profoundly. For myself, I found Fox's *Book of Martyrs* the most terrifying book I ever tried to read, not because the cruelty was greater – or indeed as great – as that committed in our own generation, but because it was done in the name of God.

A. N. Whitehead saw intolerance as 'the besetting sin of moral fervour';[1] and some of my colleagues argue that toleration of beliefs regarding God has grown as belief in God has diminished; that the religions about which men are now passionate and persecuting are the ideologies of Communism or Nazism, nationalism or race. It is a powerful argument, particularly when I, as a South African, hear talk about 'maintaining White Christian civilization' in which Christianity is identified with white supremacy, and non-racial values are asserted to be 'communist'. It is even asserted in South Africa that 'religion is concerned only with the relation between man and God, relations between men are the field of politics', and in particular, that 'religion should not concern itself with relations between groups'.

I do not think it is true to say that men grow tolerant only when they cease to believe. The Christian is not neutral.[2]

[1] A. N. Whitehead, *Adventures of Ideas* (Cambridge, 1933, paperback 1961), p. 63.

[2] Cf. Max Warren, *The Missionary Movement from Britain in Modern History* (London, 1965).

He does not see all religions as equally valid ways to God. But there is recognition of two things: first, of the truths expressed in other religions. Archbishop Temple taught that 'All that is noble in the non-Christian systems of thought or conduct or worship is the work of Christ upon them and within them . . . There is only one divine light; and every man in his measure is enlightened by it.'[1] This is the refutation of the curious idea that Christian teaching is somehow invalidated if it is not peculiar to Christianity. Some have supposed that because symbols used by Christians – death and resurrection, rebirth, virgin birth, sacrifice and communion – are used in other religions, and were used long before the birth of Christ, they are therefore invalid. Those who hold such a view forget that Christ saw himself as the fulfilment.[2] Secondly, there is a recognition that the gospel works as yeast, not law; that belief cannot be compelled; that the ultimate power is love, not force. It is evident that toleration was valued in Hindu India long before it was admitted as good in Christian Europe or in the Muslim world, and here Christians must surely acknowledge their debt to the insight of another faith.

Transcendental beliefs are a weapon which governments, whether in large- or small-scale societies, and groups within a society, continually seek to use. In the early nineteenth century Xhosa chiefs were accused of using accusations of witchcraft to rid themselves of political opponents and rivals in wealth,[3] and perhaps historians of Europe would agree that the separation of Rome and Constantinople, and the religious wars of the seventeenth century, were as much

[1] William Temple, *Readings in St John's Gospel* (London, 1940), first series, p. 101.

[2] Matthew 5:17.

[3] Wilson and Thompson, I, 269-70.

political as religious conflicts. Men were taught to think what was basically a struggle for power was a religious issue.

Cleavages expressed in theological terms commonly coincide with other cleavages in society, and what the theologian Richard Niebuhr called 'The Social Sources of Denominationalism' have been more important than is generally admitted. In the growth of Independent Churches in southern Africa, theology has been unimportant – I think very nearly irrelevant; the first splits occurred over race, as already indicated, and further splits sprang from quarrels over control of property and leadership.[1]

Christians in Africa and Asia have grown impatient of the old cleavages of Europe brought to them with Christianity itself. The Reverend Seth Mokitimi, when President of the Methodist Congress in South Africa, speaking in the Anglican cathedral in Cape Town, said: 'We were not there: we were not there when these divisions took place.' A similar impatience with the cleavages that came from Europe and were felt to be irrelevant in Africa was expressed in earlier generations by the first Xhosa minister, Tiyo Soga, and by the late Professor Jabavu.[2] The Christian Church as a whole is still in danger of being a reliquary containing the dry bones of ancient conflicts, no longer relevant but sacrosanct with age.

In every kind of society people express differences in and through religion. In our generation people express cultural,

[1] B. Sundkler, *Bantu Prophets in South Africa* (London, 1948), pp. 38-64; *Report of the Native Churches Commission*, U.G. 39, 25; *Report of Native Affairs Commission on the Israelites*, A.4-21; C. G. Oosthuizen, *Post Christianity in Africa* (London, 1968); Wilson and Mafeje, pp. 94-9.

[2] J. A. Chalmers, *The Life of Tiyo Soga* (Edinburgh, 1877), pp. 318-20; D. D. T. Jabavu, *An African Independent Church* (Lovedale, 1942).

national, racial, and class differences in the Church. With the growth of nationalism in Africa there is a danger of the growth of aggressively national Churches which might break some of their bonds with the wider Christian community as the Dutch Reformed Churches in South Africa have already done. But in every society, also, one of the functions of religion is to reconcile those who quarrel. It has been the genius of the Christian Church to bring together bond and free, Jew and Gentile, and a particular glory of the Anglican communion that it has held together and still holds together diverse groups.

Now diversity and autonomy in any society or any community or association within a wider society have a limit. If differences are too great people cannot cooperate. This applies in economic, intellectual, political, and other fields, and it applies within the Church. The question is always what *degree* of diversity and autonomy can exist. In the isolated, preliterate society there is very little, in the large society there is a great deal, as I argued in the first lecture. The plural society is an extreme form of a diverse society. So the practical problem for any organized group is what freedom to permit. The tiny Zionist groups which proliferate in South Africa achieve a very close-knit brotherhood, whose members, so far as is possible, interact only with one another. They preach no universal doctrine, and their unity is achieved by exclusiveness.[1] The warmth and mutual aid between brethren is a model to other Christians and their tendency to segment into separate and independent groups an awful warning.

The difficulty of finding a just balance between freedom and subordination applies of course to individuals as well

[1] F. B. Welbourn, *East African Rebels* (London, 1961), pp. 201-5; Wilson and Mafeje, p. 133.

as to groups. I referred in the first chapter to Maine's theme of movement from status to contract and of the evidence of growing independence of the individual as societies increased in scale. This has been one of the most thorny problems in mission congregations. The challenge to a personal, individual decision is continually put before men who, in their traditional morality, put first the welfare of the group. Contemporary missionary writers stress the responsibility of the individual to his group. The Reverend Professor John Mbiti of Makerere argues that a man cannot be Christian alone: 'So long as the individual is severed from the mass, from his kinsmen and relatives, from his community group to which he belongs by blood and culture, he will be frustrated and torn between loyalties.'[1] And Bishop Newbigin insists that 'in the great moments of the Bible when an individual is confronted with the calling of God the question at issue is never just his own destiny; it is God's purpose for his people and through them for mankind'.[2] But ultimately, for the Christian, it is the individual, not the group that is eternal. Some of you will remember the passage in *Doctor Zhivago*: 'What the Gospels tell us is that in this new way of life and of communion, which is born of the heart and which is called the Kingdom of God, there are no nations, but only persons.'[3]

The challenge to adapt society to Christian values remains, though the form of the challenge changes with time and space: the heads of the hydra are cut off but grow anew. The challenges of the affluent society are as real as the challenges of poor societies, but they are not met by a return

[1] The Rev. John Mbiti: 'The Way' and 'Means of Communicating the Gospel', in Baëta (ed.), pp. 337-8.

[2] Newbigin, p. 44.

[3] Pasternak, p. 117.

to impoverishment. The slave trade was abolished but is succeeded by colour bar, and the enormous extension in southern Africa of migratory labour. It is no answer to return to slavery, but we have to meet the problems created when inequalities are linked to visible physical differences. Inequalities in society have always been marked by differences in dress, bearing, manners, speech, and so forth, but only sometimes are they marked also by innate differences in physique. The visibility of groups in a multi-racial society complicates the building of a common society so greatly that many of my fellow whites in South Africa, and some blacks, both in Africa and America, deny it is possible. I am convinced they are wrong, but the challenge to Christians to devise the means in South Africa, in the United States, and in Britain also is obvious.

It has been argued that both transcendental religion and secular ideology determine choices in a society. Both make for the coherence of a society, and some sociologists and anthropologists have taken social coherence as an ultimate value. It cannot be the ultimate value for a Christian: the gospel in itself is revolutionary and it has been the function of the Church to change society, though repeatedly men have tried to use the Church to prevent change. Men continue to hanker after the close-knit community of the small society – and often do not understand the implications of smallness in scale. Change in stratification follows a different curve from change in scale, but the drive to egality, like the drive to increase in scale, has roots in the gospels. Resistance to increase in scale has repeatedly come from those who wield power, and again and again the Church has been identified with the privileged. The dispossessed tend to break away and form separate Churches, but we do not know why this has occurred more frequently at some periods in history than in others. The small band of believers converting their friends is the basic Christian group but some sort of organization necessarily develops to achieve continuity and unity. Nevertheless the Church cannot now embrace the whole community, for in the large society diversity is valued and the growth of toleration regarding belief about God is characteristic of the modern world. The gospel works as yeast to adapt society to Christian values.

VI. IMPLICATIONS FOR CONTEMPORARY SOCIETY: RITUAL AND CHOICE

Religion is not and never can be purely intellectual. Only an intellectual can fall into the trap of supposing it to be purely or dominantly intellectual. Ritual – the enactment of ultimate beliefs – comprehends more than is understood. It includes the whole man, subconscious as well as conscious, and always has in it an element of mystery. The celebration of ritual expresses unconscious desires and attitudes of the participants, and helps to make them conscious.

In small, preliterate societies ritual is the dominant element in religion. Theology, the intellectual element, develops with increase of scale, most notably with writing, and with the growth of universities.

Our contemporary society is enjoying a golden age of science. The dazzling achievements of natural scientists ensure that the emphasis during the last three centuries has been on the intellectual aspect of society; on understanding. The Reformation was characterized by a growing distrust of ritual, and a fear lest it substitute for thinking. This was particularly marked in Scotland and was accompanied by enormous emphasis on education. These tendencies were reflected in mission fields in Africa in the nineteenth and twentieth centuries, especially in missions of the Reformed Churches.[1] But of course theology never replaces worship any more than science replaces poetry. Both are required for the full development of persons and communities. Where there is no outlet for emotion in a liturgy the stress

[1] F. B. Welbourn, 'A Note on Types of Religious Society', in Baëta (ed.), p. 138.

is likely to be on revivalism, with sermons aimed at rousing emotion.[1]

The efficacy of ritual springs from the fact that it represents eternal realities: birth, maturity, death, family relations, neighbourly relations, love and hate. During periods of very rapid social change there appears to be a loss of consciousness of the meaning of traditional symbols, even when old forms are followed. Furthermore, old symbols become inappropriate if tied to a particular economy – hunting, pastoral, or agricultural – or a particular social structure. Animal sacrifice may be appropriate for a herdsman but not for a townsman, and the crown, for so long a potent symbol in monarchies, is not appropriate in a republic.

The occasions of ritual are constant as we have seen: birth, maturity, marriage, death, public crises or rejoicing. The individual, torn by feeling, needs help. He needs to be taught what to feel and how to express it. He needs help in accepting the death of someone close, in realizing death and turning again to life, rather than pretending it has not happened. The adolescent, or the bride and groom, or the young mother, or widowed man or woman, all have to learn to accept a change in status. It is no accident that so many people who do not attend Church nevertheless seek the services of the Church for marriages, christenings, and funerals. Those who feel that to do so would be hypocrisy may nevertheless express a deep longing for some appropriate ritual to help them through. To refuse to celebrate any ritual at a crisis is in a sense a denial of dependence upon one's fellows; it is a withdrawal into oneself, an assertion that one chooses to be alone in grief or joy.

In Africa I have found greater constancy in what is ex-

[1] Cf. William James, *The Varieties of Religious Experience* (London, 1902), *passim.*

pressed than in the forms of expression: that is, in the attitudes which people are required to express than in the symbols used. The Nyakyusa were aware of this. A young clerk, Mwaisumo, pointed out that details of ritual varied with lineage among the half million of Nyakyusa-speakers and neighbours who spoke other languages; and that what food was used depended on the local economy. On the Lake shore fish was used, in the middle belt bananas, in the drier upland beans, and so on. The similarities between the funeral rites or puberty rites of the various groups was recognized, and the similarities in what was expressed repeatedly asserted, though detailed differences in custom were followed. In Europe it has been argued that symbols remained constant though the meaning changed; that when St Augustine of Canterbury baptized 'the fanes' he charged old symbols and old places with new meaning. It is not for an anthropologist, ignorant of theology, to question this, but I do ask whether, *at some level*, there was not continuity of content as well as of form; rebirth and renewal are themes which did not originate in Christian ritual.

The growing point of ritual in Africa is in the Independent Churches. Every Independent Church elaborates ritual further than the Church from which it sprang, and in what emerges there is the fusion of diverse traditions. In the rituals of Zionist Churches of Zululand there are combined the meat offering of Bantu Africa with the flowers and bananas of India, and the cross and some of the vestments of Christian tradition.[1]

A Lutheran missionary in South Africa, the Reverend Hans Haselbarth, wrote recently that 'Christianity tried to send its roots down into the African mind but was satisfied

[1] A-I. Berglund, *Rituals of an African Bantu Church*, University of the Witwatersrand, Occasional Papers 3, pp. 1-2.

with only a section of it, namely that of reason and progress'. He finds much of the popular symbolism, particularly the funeral rites, pagan. 'Death and funeral rites are the broad highway on which a new kind of paganism forces its entry into congregations.'[1] But the hunger for symbolism is plain. Indeed the wake, when 'the living entertain for their lost relatives' is a major social occasion for Christians both in African townships and in the country, just as the pagan funeral feast for 'bringing home the shade' (*ukubuyisa ekhaya*) was in traditional African societies.

Problems of translation in time and space are not new in the Christian Church; they were there between Hebrew and Greek, Europe and Africa, or the medieval world and the twentieth century. There are failures of communication between generations and classes, as well as between peoples of different language and nationality. Dr Visser T'Hooft spoke not long ago of the narrow passage between syncretism and failure to interpret in local or contemporary terms,[2] and often those who are closest to a traditional pagan background are most insistent on the need to use new symbols to express new conceptions. When I first worked among the Nyakyusa before the last war, I reflected somewhat critically on the fact that missionaries had not used the common foods of the country – millet beer, and bananas or beans – for the communion feast, but the foods of the Mediterranean – wine and wheaten bread. And then I found that an Independent Church, unable to obtain wine, and having difficulty in obtaining wheat, nevertheless used *new* rather than traditional foods for the communion. They filled the com-

[1] Hans Haselbarth, 'Why seek Ye the Living among the Dead?', *Ministry* (Morija), July 1966.

[2] Visser T'Hooft, 'Modernizing without Compromising', *The Listener*, 9 March 1967, p. 327.

munion cup with tea, and offered rice. The break with the past was felt necessary. Furthermore, to many Africans it is the universality of Christianity that is so important and local diversities in ritual may endanger it. It is a cogent argument, but it has not precluded Rome from finally following other communions in translating the mass into the vernacular. Perhaps there is always a choice between universality in time and space and intelligibility to ordinary people.

You will remember that Pope Gregory the Great sent a message after St Augustine at Canterbury telling him that he should not destroy the old temples but purify them.[1] Uncertainty whether destruction or reform is the right policy in any particular case is still with us. Symbols spring out of familiar earth and men crave for the poetry of home, but new ideas and circumstances may require new symbols.

Rituals cannot be invented. Their impact is partly due to their antiquity or even timelessness. New symbols may well up from the subconscious and 'catch on', in the way in which a new poem or song catches on because it expresses what the hearers feel; but equally, the new symbol or rite

[1] 'I have, upon mature deliberation on the affair of the English determined . . . that the temples of idols in that nation ought not to be destroyed; but let the idols that are in them be destroyed; let holy water be made and sprinkled in the said temples, let altars be erected, and relics placed. For if those temples are well built it is requisite that they be converted from the worship of devils to the service of the true God; that the nation, seeing that their temples are not destroyed, may remove error from their hearts, and knowing and adoring the true God, may the more familiarly resort to the places to which they have been accustomed. And because they have been used to slaughter many oxen in the sacrifice to devils, some solemnity must be exchanged for them on this account, as that on the day of the dedication, or the nativities of the holy martyres, whose relics are there deposited, they may build themselves huts of the boughs of trees, about those churches that have turned to that use from temples, and celebrate the solemnity with religious feasting.' The Venerable Bede, *Ecclesiastical History*, I, Chapter 30 (edited J. A. Giles, London, 1847).

may *not* catch on. It is felt to be meaningless or irrelevant.

The problem of how ritual can be both relevant to contemporary life and have the sense of timelessness which is a source of its strength, is wider than the problem of how Christianity can be expressed in the idioms of another language and people. Can ritual exist in a rapidly changing society? I am certain that it can and must because what it expresses is, at the deepest level, constant; it is the acceptance of birth and death, of growth and change, of the dependence of man on God. The last point, dependence of man on God, is where I part company with many of my colleagues who see man as self-sufficient, master of his fate.

But in fact, wherever men deny the existence of a transcendental god they fashion a new god, and appeal to that image, whether a historical process or an ideal society, or whatever it may be. 'History will absolve me', says Castro; 'History will avenge him', cries Tariq Ali, speaking of Che Guevara.[1] What is expressed shows remarkable continuity, but understanding of what is to be expressed, and of the symbols used, has to be achieved in each generation. When a society is changing very fast this is difficult. Symbols familiar and conscious to one generation becomes a 'forgotten language' to another, as I have shown (p. 72).

In the first chapter, I argued that with increase in scale there is a growth of self-awareness (self-consciousness). There is expression of self – of man and his relations with men and with the universe, with his fellow-men and his gods – in the simplest societies, and when the rituals of the preliterate peoples are unravelled they reveal a profound knowledge of men's minds and hearts; of the corroding power of hatred and unbridled lust, of the necessity of confession of these if a man is to free himself from them; of the

[1] Tariq Ali, 'Gods and Guerrillas', *Punch*, 13 November 1968.

recurrent need in every individual to break with his past and begin anew. Some ask themselves whether a hunter in the forest or the desert, or a preliterate Nyakyusa was not more self-aware than we are, and particularly not more aware of himself as a member of a group. I am sure he was not. The measure of self-consciousness in a Nyakyusa ritual seems to me much less than in Shakespeare's plays, the novels of Tolstoy, or the Italian painters of the Renaissance. The range of awareness is much more limited: the complexity of personalities, and the infinite variations in interaction is not expressed.

Furthermore, in small societies man's self-consciousness is largely confined to the arts: myth, story, song, sculpture, painting. With modern man has come the flowering of science, the study of the universe and of man's relationship with man through the physical, biological, and social sciences. Our knowledge of man in society has lagged far behind our knowledge of the physical structure of the universe, perhaps because it is more complex, and perhaps because we have been more fearful of studying it. Nevertheless there has been a great advance during the last hundred years in man's knowledge of himself. The theory of evolution as expounded by Darwin, the conception of the unconscious expounded by Freud, and the idea of a growth in self-consciousness elaborated by Teilhard de Chardin: these are landmarks in the process whereby man is beginning to analyse himself and his relationships with other men, as well as to interpret himself and his group symbolically. The arts and sciences are complementary approaches to the understanding of self, of man in his environment both physical and social, and with the rapid growth of knowledge in the last two generations we have begun to catch up in the intellectual aspect with an *awareness* that was already foreshadowed in preliterate societies in the symbolic aspect. A full self-consciousness will only be achieved through both.

Sometimes it is suggested that knowledge and awareness, analysis and symbol, are somehow incompatible: that any dissection of symbols by an artist leads to the atrophy of his creative talent. But the self-consciousness which is lethal to art is surely not that reflective thought about which Teilhard was talking, but a self-centredness in which the artist concerned is deflected from reality by preoccupation with technique, when he lets exhibition of skill take command over what he seeks to express. For self-understanding man requires both the intellectual formulation and the image, and the pervasive feeling of lostness is partly due to the loss of awareness of traditional symbols during rapid change. The old symbols are no longer felt to be relevant, and men grope after appropriate images to express their relationships with God and man; they are feeling after new images of God.[1]

One of the continuing needs in any society is an appropriate imagery through which men may achieve some measure of self-consciousness, and as the material form and intellectual understanding of a society change the imagery necessarily changes also. And so, as civilization develops (and ultimately civilization is one, not many), art develops also, drawing on new skills and new knowledge, continually seeking appropriate images. Sometimes it enjoys a golden age when men rejoice in their ability to feel and express; today it is natural science which is in its golden age and we marvel at the strides in knowledge and fear an atrophy of the arts. This, I think, is temporary: a man walking moves only one foot at a time. Already there are signs that in the present student generation talent is flowing strongly towards the arts and social studies. Professor Levi-Strauss'

[1] Cf. A. C. Bridge, *Images of God* (London, 1960).

influence in anthropology is partly due to his stress on the symbolic aspect, to his passion for understanding wholes.

Self-awareness is never complete. To be born into a society in which the meaning of symbols is conscious to many assists the individual to achieve a measure of self-consciousness, but does not ensure it.

One obvious point emerges from the consideration of large-scale societies. If freedom of conscience is admitted, communal rituals, celebrated on behalf of a community or nation, cannot be obligatory, and where the society is very diverse, it is unlikely that a communal ritual will even command the assent of everyone. Those of us who are non-conformists in the countries in which we live fear the compulsory celebration of communal rituals to which we cannot subscribe as, for example, celebrations in South Africa which glorify the conquest by whites.

The dilemma was obvious in Great Britain at the time of the abdication of Edward VIII when it was impossible for the Archbishop of Canterbury to celebrate the coronation ritual, but many ordinary citizens felt that it was not for the Church to dictate to the nation who should, or should not, become king. At the same time many people argued that it would be a pity if the coronation ceased to be a ritual, and became a purely secular ceremonial. This brings us to the heart of the matter: ordinary people crave for the endorsement of important occasions by some power beyond themselves, and beyond the government they elect.

It was shown in the third chapter that in traditional African societies rituals were occasions for *speaking out*, for bringing into the open quarrels which were festering, for admission of anger was believed to be necessary for reconciliation. Connor Cruise O'Brien suggested recently that the United Nations fulfills this function.[1] The 'speaking out' in the United Nations Assembly often shocks Western diplomats who argue that the expression of extreme views makes reconciliation more difficult, but it is directly in line with traditional rituals in Africa.

Furthermore, the ethologists suggest that forms of aggressive display which become innate in certain biological species are a *substitute* for attack.[2] O'Brien writes: 'The United Nations performs the function of providing great powers with an alternative and sacrosanct means of preserving their dignity on the world stage in conditions where the normal means of preserving dignity – that of adhering to a consistent course – would carry them and the world over the brink of war.' The United Nations is seen as 'an imaginative release for human emotions and ritual substitute for destructive human activities'.[3]

In both international and national spheres men are groping after symbols which command loyalty, and rituals which will reconcile conflicting parties. In national states the most usual common symbols are flag and national anthem, but there are others also. The search for secular symbols which will be acceptable in states with diverse populations and religions is oddly reflected in postage stamps. The stamps I collected in my youth mostly showed crowned heads or presidents. Today I notice not only national heroes (who can be controversial if they were political leaders) but natural features of the country like mountains, or the flowers, wild animals, and birds which everyone can admire, great works of art, or the products of the country which require advertise-

[1] Connor Cruise O'Brien, *The United Nations: Sacred Drama* (Hutchinson, 1968).

[2] Lorentz, p. 56.

[3] Christopher Serpell, 'Golden Bough over the East River', *The Listener*, 30 May 1968.

ment. Cattle reappear on the stamps of cattle-owners in Africa who once sacrificed them to their shades.

Separation between Church and state, between the community of believers and the political unit, is inevitable in a large-scale society and a condition of freedom of conscience. I do not regard the separation as something to be regretted. It is also evident that some states, notably Britain, have separated ceremonial office in the state from legislative power, but in France and the United States this has not been achieved. Separation of ceremonial and legislative functions is comparable to the separation of judicial and legislative functions and is surely the mark of a highly-developed political structure. Where the offices are fused power is more absolute and one individual may be overwhelmed with work. Where the ceremonial office is ancient and hereditary its very antiquity creates an aura of authority – the majesty so assiduously cultivated in African chiefdoms by the use of medicines.[1] Newly-invented ceremonial usually appears somewhat ridiculous.

Nowhere can the Church now claim to celebrate rituals which are obligatory for the citizens of the state, though it does provide a regular order of service and special occasions for Christian citizens who pray for their country. The United States of America have never had a national Church but God is still invoked by the President at times of national crisis and at the annual festivals celebrating Thanksgiving, Independence, and Washington's birthday. Professor Bellah calls this 'civil religion'.[2] The characteristic is that dependence of the national state on God is expressed, and belief

[1] M. Wilson, *Communal Rituals*, pp. 57-63.

[2] R. N. Bellah, 'Religious Evolution', *American Sociological Review*, **29** (1964), 358-86; 'Civil Religion in America', *Daedalus*, **96**, 1 (1967), 1-21.

in God is still sufficiently widespread in the United States for such expression to be a force for national cohesion rather than a ground of conflict.

The question that concerns Christians is: granted that ritual remains as a necessary expression of our relationships with God and man, are the forms used in the Church appropriate to contemporary society? I don't know the answer to that, but I have read H. A. Williams'[1] criticism of existing rituals with great interest, and in listening to innumerable sermons on the sin of not attending Church I am reminded of pagan Xhosa talking about the necessity of observing *amasiko*, that is, celebrating traditional sacrifices. There is a nagging suspicion that Christian rituals may also be regarded as obligatory *because* they are traditional, rather than because they are the most appropriate form for expressing certain attitudes.

I have argued the necessity for ritual in the life of the individual when crises occur, and to me the frequent communion feast is irreplaceable. It brings together God and man, and man and man, whether living or dead, poor or rich, young or old. But I accept that many of my friends do not find this and that they seek expression rather in music or painting, poetry or drama or architecture. 'Bach is God' is a familiar slogan, painted on a wall in Oxford. But note that someone who argued, 'Bach *is* religion to me', nevertheless sang in a church choir: the music that meant so much to her was composed for worship. All the arts[2] have of course been fostered by religion, and an art may wither when the religion of which it was handmaid loses conviction. This is

[1] Vidler (ed.), *Soundings*, pp. 79ff.

[2] Even landscape gardening, which was developed in China and Japan in relation to temples.

true of sculpture in much of Africa where it was linked very closely with the cult of the shades.

The perennial tension is between form and spiritual content. God is a spirit and Christians seek to worship in spirit and in truth: they seek to shed magic, that is reliance on the particular and material form. But they cannot escape form any more than thought can escape words, and like words, the form must serve to communicate between contemporaries and between generations.

In considering translation, I ask myself what are the special insights in traditional African religion that may contribute to an African interpretation of Christianity, and through African congregations to the universal Church.[1] Looking back on all I have learnt in Africa from village men and women expounding law and custom, four ideas impress themselves. In much of Africa men pondered on man's relationship with man, rather than on the nature of God. The cult of the shades reflects a lively sense that kinsmen are members one of another in time and space. Community has narrow limits, but it does not stop at death. Responsibility is recognized both to the dead and the unborn.

This community of living and dead is something the West may relearn. Given the climate of our time we are slow to mention mystical experience, but to some who have spent their lives aware of that dependence upon the shades which characterizes most of Africa, the findings of the Society for Psychical Research confirm what we already know. The dead live; they are concerned with those who were close to

[1] Cf. Kwesi Dickson and Paul Ellingworth, *Biblical Revelation and African Beliefs* (London, 1969).

them in life; love is not extinguished.[1] But men have struggled free from the tight bonds of kin, and cease to fear the dead as a source of personal misfortune.

In Africa there has been a keen awareness that the sin of one affects others: that the sins of the fathers are visited on the children, and that a breach of obligations may bring disaster on all. The obligations are pictured in magical terms: widow or widower may not remarry before purification is complete, and a twin must be buried in wet earth, or drought will engulf the chiefdom – but the underlying notion of mutual responsibility within a community is profoundly true. Parents are in some measure responsible for delinquent children, and ignorant or greedy methods of farming by some create a dustbowl which others must endure. Dr Kenneth Kaunda, the President of Zambia, once wrote that Africa's gift was in human relationships, and in so far as there are differences between groups of people, I think this is true. But note one difficulty: a sense of community, of mutual aid and responsibility, is harder to achieve in a large-scale society than in a small-scale one, and the small-scale society is constricting in a way in which those who have not lived in it scarcely realize. The problem is to combine the warmth of a small community with the freedom of the large society; to move from a kin-bound world – kin-bound in time as well as space – to the divine commonwealth where we may be fellow-citizens with the saints. We must not confuse what is attributable to smallness of scale with what may be specifically African insights.

Secondly, men in Africa were aware of the reality of evil. They were indeed similarly aware in medieval Europe, but

[1] Rosalind Heywood, 'Attitudes to death in the light of dreams and other out of body experience', 'Death and Psychical Research', in *Man's Concern with Death*, Arnold Toynbee *et al.* (London, 1968).

westerners have half forgotten this since the idea of progress came into the saddle. In Africa evil was seen as anger, hate, envy, and greed festering within men, unconfessed, bottled up, and in one area after another we find a stress on *speaking out*, on confession of anger and hate, for it is thought that reconciliation can only follow the admission of evil thoughts. The devil as pictured in Christian tradition is a symbol which has ceased to seem appropriate to many Christians: to me it is no more appropriate than the Nyakyusa conception of a python in the belly of a witch, or the Xhosa idea of a baboon ridden backwards by his witch master – but though the devil with horns is ludicrous, evil is not: it is fearful. And Africans are not so far out as was thought a hundred years ago when they argue that anger and hate, envy and greed bring sickness: that good health ultimately depends upon good social relationships. A psychosomatic element is present in all disease.[1]

Are we thinking hard enough now about curing people of evil? About arming them against it? The Christian knows he cannot build Utopia on earth but it is his business to work for the sort of society which will not cause his fellow to stumble. There are social conditions that *breed* delinquents. The evidence from primate studies is that what makes a monkey unable to adjust is deprivation from the mother or isolation from playmates,[2] and that crowding produces violence.[3] Paediatricians recognize a 'maternal deprivation syndrome' in which a child fails to grow not because of lack

[1] D. Stafford Clark, *Psychiatry for Students* (2nd edn, London, 1966), p. 134.

[2] H. F. Harlow and M. K. Harlow, 'Social Deprivation in Monkeys', *Scientific American*, November 1962, 136-46.

[3] C. Russell and W. M. S. Russell, *Violence, Monkeys and Man* (London, 1968), *passim.*

of food, but purely because it is given insufficient love and attention by its mother.

In human communities the absence of a father creates further difficulties in bringing up children. The widespread separation of families, husbands being forced to live away from wives and children, characterized slavery in the Southern States of America, and such separation is now far more extensive under the system of migrant labour in South Africa. It is the official policy of my country that African men should find employment in towns and on white-owned farms, but leave their wives and families in reserves. It is comparable to a *permanent* situation of war, when more than half the able-bodied men are away on service at any one time, and it disrupts a society, bequeathing a legacy of disorder to succeeding generations.

Aggression may be fostered or limited by the structure of the society. Men in very small societies are not all given to warfare. The hunters and gatherers who still exist in parts of southern and central Africa are not warlike,[1] nor were the Eskimo, though Indian hunting groups in South America were.[2] The institutions and values of the society are factors at least as important as innate characteristics in determining how aggression is expressed or controlled.

Thirdly, competition was bridled in Africa. Competition is so built into our system of education that we take it for granted, but it surely has got out of hand.

Lorentz tell us that the 'working pace of civilized man is one of the errors of evolution'.[3] That pleased me, particularly, coming from a scholar living in Germany. Dr

[1] E. Thomas, *The Harmless People* (London, 1959); Turnbull, *The Forest People*.

[2] Francis Huxley, *Affable Savages* (London, n.d.), p. 95.

[3] Lorentz, p. 139.

Kaunda talks about 'the success–failure complex' as being a 'disease of civilization', and he drives it to the point of insisting that there should be no university failures in Zambia. How far this is compatible with maintaining academic standards remains to be seen, but if one of the needs of our society is to learn again to *be still*, then we can look for instruction in Africa. I remember returning to South Africa after six months in the United States and in London and noticing, directly I landed, the change in *pace*, and above all the total relaxation of Africans lying on the grass during the lunch hour.

Fourthly, traditions in Africa provide a balance to the intellectual emphasis of the West. There has been an apprehension of reality through ritual rather than dogma, and scientific answers are still regarded as partial answers. In the West the respect for natural science deflects us from asking certain fundamental questions because natural science cannot deal with them. It cannot answer the question the Mpondo or Nyakyusa is primarily concerned with when his child dies: 'Why did it happen to me?' 'Who caused it?'

In the field of medicine, scientific understanding and imaginative apprehension are much closer than they used to be. A few months ago a review of Stephen Black's *Mind and Body* suggested that 'in some cases the virus seems to be little more than the agent obeying the mind's commands'.[1] Reading that I felt I was back in Pondoland with the teacher who asked 'Who sent the louse?'

Science cannot answer many questions that poets in the Western world are still asking. Simone de Beauvoir wrote in *A Very Easy Death*, 'There is no such thing as a natural death: . . . but for every man his death is an accident and,

[1] Brian Inglis, 'Uncharted Regions', *Punch*, 7 May 1969.

even if he knows it and consents to it, an unjustifiable violation.'[1]

Perhaps it is because science cannot answer 'Who sent the louse?' 'Why did it happen to me?' that many in the contemporary world try to ignore death. Mr Gorer tells us death is no longer mentioned in polite conversation though birth and sex are now discussed as they were not in Victorian times.[2] In England people play down grief, they ignore traditional symbols of mourning, they curtail funerals.[3] Perhaps even the so-called 'American way of death' is an attempt to avoid mourning by paying.[4] The contrast between the exuberance of mourning in traditional Africa and Victorian England, and contemporary England is radical.

Death remains. There is no answer to why evil exists, but evil accepted was the supreme revelation of good.[5] Acceptance of death is very different from trying to pretend it does not exist.

I have spoken of what we can learn from old Africa, but there are also new problems, peculiar to the contemporary world. Some are obvious and need not delay us long. Fertility was an ultimate value down through Africa and perhaps in most of the world. That value is now an anachronism, and the implications that it is out of date are only partially accepted. Population may overwhelm us. The danger of too many people for the land and resources available was recognized by some preliterate groups, notably the Tikopian

[1] Simone de Beauvoir, *A Very Easy Death* (translated, Patrick O'Brian, Harmondsworth, 1969), p. 92.

[2] C. Gorer, *Death, Grief and Mourning* (London, 1965), p. 111.

[3] Gorer, *passim*.

[4] E. Waugh, *The Loved One* (London, 1948).

[5] H. A. Williams, *The Suffering of Mankind* (Coventry, 5 December 1966).

islanders,[1] but many groups in Africa were struggling to maintain themselves, to maintain their numbers in the face of disease or drought. When a certain variety of aphids reach a given point of crowding they grow wings and a colony flies off. Perhaps men will also take off as crowding grows, but science offers other choices: we may choose to limit population and plan for new kinds of cities.

A second problem is the *pace* of change – in what Dr Leach called 'the runaway world'. Harmony between successive generations is always something rather difficult to achieve. The range of preliterate societies reflects innumerable experiments in how to order relationships between fathers and sons, mothers and daughters, so that the adjustments necessary when sons and daughters change from helpless infants to adults could be made. My Nyakyusa friends even went to the point of insisting that fathers and sons should live in separate *villages*; they must never live close to one another, according to Nyakyusa ideas, and little boys began to build apart from their fathers when they were eight or nine. So generation conflict is nothing new. What *is* new is the change in manner of life, now so great within one generation that a son's ideas and symbols and values are necessarily considerably different from those of his father. A son would not pass his university examinations if he served up the ideas his father was taught; he would be inefficient in his profession, unemployable as a technician, and so on. The difficulty is increased by the longer expectation of life. The young grow impatient at the delay in achieving power, and the old may suffer unemployment or feel neglected. The far-reaching effects of changes in the expectation of life are as yet scarcely explored. In parts of

[1] Raymond Firth, *Primitive Polynesian Economy* (London, 1939), pp. 32-77.

East and Central Africa relations between generations were governed by the celebration of a great ritual, every thirty years, at which power was handed over by the old to the young.[1] That system had drawbacks – among the Nyakyusa it included the practice of smothering the chief if he did not die quickly – and it really is not very convenient if all the experienced administrators – even all the professors in a university – retire at once. But what we can learn from Africa is the value of dramatizing change in the life of the individual, teaching old as well as young, to *expect* different positions in society; and defining their new functions.

The difficulty experienced by individuals in accepting their roots when they live through a period of radical change has been familiar in the United States which received so many immigrants from very different social environments and turned them into one-hundred-per-cent Americans.[2] It is familiar in Africa where the son of an illiterate man in an isolated tribal society may emerge as a university graduate, travelling in the one world of today.

In a world in which the pace of change continuously accelerates, men become bewildered. Stiffly, creakingly, each generation tries to adapt itself to this giddy pace and forgets the difficulties of its fathers. Professor Erik Erikson in *Insight and Responsibility* illuminates the problems of the man who must accept his roots but adapt to the new society. The personal difficulties of the Jewish immigrant from Eastern Europe who prospered in the United States is brilliantly analysed. If he rejects his roots – his subconscious – he loses his personal integrity. The search for identity, according to Erikson, must include self-realization in

[1] M. Wilson, *Communal Rituals*, pp. 49-57; *Good Company*, pp. 22-31.

[2] M. Mead, . . . *And Keep Your Powder Dry* (U.S.A., 1942, English edition, *The American Character*, Pelican, 1944).

identification with parent, overcoming the guilt at the rejection of parents that follows in adolescence, and acceptance of a new independent person.[1]

The search for identity is not purely an individual matter, for a man realizes himself as a member of a group, or nowadays of several groups – a family, a profession, a church or political party, a school or university, and a state. Both men and communities – individuals and groups – must respect their own past or they fall sick of the conflicts within them. The present preoccupation with history in Africa is thus no accident; it is part of the growth of a national consciousness wider than old tribal loyalties. Anthropology is usually rejected by the young nationalists because it is felt to represent a static past – it seems to savour of the zoo or the game reserve. But there is a passionate desire to link the past with the present; to understand the process of development.

The reality of uprootedness is distorted in two ways: the first distortion constantly preached to Africans in South Africa by whites is that a people can only 'develop on their own lines'. This ignores the fact that every civilization has been built by borrowing from others. The second distortion is an aggressive jingoism, an assertion of exclusive nationalism.

The idea of national growth and identity has nowhere been more fully understood than in England. I listened, as a very raw student, to lectures on English constitutional history in King's College, and came away with the conviction that no institution existed in England which did not have roots going back at least to Anglo-Saxon times. Political institutions had grown as a tree grows from the seed. That understanding has given generations of Englishmen great assurance. They could accept change and development with-

[1] Erikson, *Insight and Responsibility*, pp. 83-107.

out feeling there was any break with the past. But if identity is sought in a very narrow and exclusive nationalism then men fear to change one jot or tittle of the law.

The Church looks back to an event, the death and resurrection of Jesus, which it seeks to interpret to each generation, and the forms it provides in which men express their faith are mostly traditional; ritual constantly derives sanctity from antiquity as has been shown. But the gospel is revolutionary and revolution today lies in the exercise of choice.

Increase in scale means *increase in freedom of choice*. The individual and the group are less and less circumscribed by physical necessity as science and technology provide control of the material environment. This strikes home to anyone who lives for a time with preliterate people, especially with hunters and gatherers whose resources are very limited, and for whom life is altogether precarious.

As was noted in the first chapter, the development of medical science means that man is less circumscribed by biological necessity. Both disease and conception can be controlled. Man has wealth and skill and can choose how to use them.[1] And finally, in the large-scale, diverse society man is less circumscribed by social custom: he has a choice of home, job, friends, of recreation, of religious belief and practice that is not there in the small society.

Choices press hardest on leaders. It is those who have most gifts – ability, wealth, status – for whom the choice is widest, and whose choices most affect others. The mobile man moving from one position to another in society – as an African from an illiterate family who achieves higher education, or an Englishman who grows up poor and wins the

[1] Cf. *South African Outlook*, February 1967, editorial p. 17.

pools – is beset with choices for which his own family tradition provides no precedents. Many of my friends have found the choices open to them almost overwhelming: had they been less gifted, more circumscribed perhaps by pressing financial necessity, more closely tied by birth and kinship obligations as a pagan Nyakyusa was, then life would have been simpler. They would have known what to do. It is often the most gifted boy who finds it hardest to choose a profession, and the difficulty of choosing may disrupt him. The less gifted have fewer choices open to them. Freedom may also be very lonely. In a small society companionship is provided for by the network of kinship and age-mates. In a large society one chooses one's friends.

Now choice is determined by values, and values must relate to one's conception of ultimate reality, to what I have defined as transcendental religion or secular ideology.

A magical arbiter of choice is still constantly sought by divination. The popular current form is to consult the stars and cast a horoscope. In theory choices are made in terms of place and date of birth in relation to the movement of the constellations – ascertainable facts – but the interpretations, the deductions drawn, are at least as subjective as interpretations of the Zande ordeal, or bones thrown by a Sotho diviner. Readership of the astrological columns of British papers and magazines is asserted to be 'at least twenty-six million', surely evidence of an intense and unsatisfied craving for guidance in choice.

To the Christian a *magical* solution of choice – the expectation of some sign – becomes less and less acceptable as the obligation to love with one's mind is explored. Of course many people go on asking for signs as Christ predicted they would.[1] Another popular form of evading choice is to

[1] John 4:48.

follow a leader and leave all choices to him. Collectivism is an alternative to magic.

Bonhoeffer[1] talked about bringing God back into the centre of life. He argued that God is not a residual explanation, the cause of those phenomena that the scientist cannot yet explain, or the doctor, the engineer, the social scientist control, but the centre. Surely God is the centre as the arbiter, the touchstone of choice. As choice grows man's need for guidance becomes greater and greater. Salvation for the Christian implies the courage to choose. The function of the Church is to help men to choose. Choice has an intellectual element – the weighing up of *pros* and *cons*, the assessment of right and wrong. And specialists in the study of social institutions – economists, anthropologists, sociologists, lawyers – have a role in indicating the implications of certain choices.[2] But choice is partly intuitive, and intuitive choice is nourished in ritual. A habit of mind is formed which guides choice, in the same sort of way as taste is trained in the study of literature, or music, or painting.

The most fearful choice of all is that of life or death. How do we interpret the gospels in contemporary terms to guide a doctor when facing this choice? How do we exercise love in the preservation of life? In traditional Nyakyusa thought the worst thing that could happen to a man was 'not to be able to die' (*akamanya ukufwa*). It was the punishment of sin, a fate worse than death. And a due time for death was recognized. Sometimes a man would say '*Ngatele nsumwike*' – 'I'm tired, I'm going'. Listening to my medical colleagues talk I find them agreed on one point: dying in hospital nowadays is an unpleasant, undignified, and undesirable

[1] D. Bonhoeffer, *Letters and Papers from Prison* (English translation, London, 1953).

[2] Godfrey Wilson, 'Anthropology as a Public Service', *Africa*, 13 (1940), pp. 45-59.

way to go. Life drags on too long when all the modern techniques are applied. Is quality not relevant? Is there not a proper term to life? If so, how do we define it? Pneumonia used to be known as 'the old man's friend': who should decide whether he may visit? What of the patient who does not wish to be resuscitated?[1] And what are the criteria when choosing which life to preserve? – Shaw's *Doctor's Dilemma* is still before us, only now we discuss it in terms of renal failure, transplants, and machines, rather than tuberculosis and a sanitorium. When resources are limited and it comes to a choice of whom to keep alive, are not the old expendable rather than the young, the less fit rather than the more fit? Such choices have regularly been made in hunting communities when the old and sometimes the very young had to be left behind if the band was to survive.

To some of us the essential meaning of the virgin birth is that it symbolizes a deliberate choice and acceptance. To quote Pasternak again: 'She [Mary] gives birth not of necessity but by a miracle, by an inspiration. And from now on the basis of life is no longer to be compulsion, it is to be that very same inspiration – this is what the New Testament offers . . . the unusual instead of the commonplace, the festive instead of the workaday, inspiration instead of compulsion.'[2]

Choice is there whether we define it in religious or secular terms. I claim as an ally in this argument my atheist friend and colleague, Dr Leach, for in his Reith Lectures he hammered home the need to accept choice, the need to make responsible choices.

Increase in choice implies an increased potentiality

[1] A. Paton, 'A Personal View', *British Medical Journal*, 6 September 1969, p. 591.

[2] Pasternak, p. 370.

for both good and evil. Man may become more fully human, or he may pursue evil. St Augustine, the African, talks about the 'abysmal depths of personality'. The Christian belief is that God gives men power to choose right. We say with St Paul 'but the evil which I would not that I do',[1] and seek help. St John speaks of men who believe in the Word made Flesh being given power to become sons of God.[2] Of course the choices may not be comfortable, for the God who returns to the centre is the suffering servant and no magician. There are no magical solutions to our individual or social discontents. It is the scientist who disposes of force. But wrestling with the choices is part of loving God with our minds.

There remains a paradox and it is a paradox because our understanding is so limited. As anthropologists well know, it is when hypotheses are inadequate that contradictions are inexplicable. I have argued that the movement in society is towards the personal, towards a growing self-awareness: that this can be traced in biological evolution and that it is visible also in societies with what Maine called the movement from status to contract. Such growth towards the personal fits with Christ's teaching on the nature of God: 'Are not two sparrows sold for a farthing? And one of them shall not fall on the ground without your Father. But the very hairs of your head are all numbered.'[3] Biological and social evidence and revelation confirm one another. If the whole movement of history is towards the personal it cannot, I believe, stop at death. Christ asserted it did not, and personal survival, which so many in my generation think inconceivable, finds confirmation in this reading of human

[1] Romans 7:19.
[2] John 1:12.
[3] Matthew 10:29f.

development. But the larger the society the more important do impersonal relationships become, and scientific thinking has been fostered by this very growth of impersonal relations. How can impersonal and personal *both* develop? And a further paradox lies in the combination of the personal and innumerable; of infinities of time and space and a man as a unique personality. I cannot probe this mystery or pretend to understand. It is outside time, beyond space, part of 'That heavenly city which has Truth for its King, Love for its Law, and Eternity for its Measure'.[1]

[1] St Augustine, *The City of God* (translated John Healey, London, 1931), p. xii.

BIBLIOGRAPHY

BOOKS

Arkel, A. J. *A History of the Sudan to 1821*, London, 1955.

Baëta, C. G. *Christianity in Tropical Africa*, London, 1968.

Bede, The Venerable. *Ecclesiastical History*, edited J. A. Giles, London, 1847.

Biéler, A. *The Social Humanism of Calvin*, English translation, Richmond, Virginia, 1964.

Bleek, D. *The Naron*, Cambridge, 1928.

Bokwe, J. K. *Ntsikana*, Lovedale, 1914.

Bonhoeffer, D. *Letters and Papers from Prison*, English translation, London, 1953.

Bridge, A. C. *Images of God*, London, 1960.

Brown, J. T. *Among the Bantu Nomads*, London, 1926.

Brown, Peter, *Augustine of Hippo*, London, 1967.

Bunyan, J. *The Pilgrim's Progress*, London, 1672.

Loeto loa Mokereseti, Tswana translation, Kuruman, 1848.

Uhambo Lomhambi, Xhosa translation by Tiyo Soga, Lovedale, 1866.

Butterfield, Herbert. *Christianity in European History*, London, 1951.

Callaway, The Rev. Canon. *The Religious System of the Amazulu*, Cape Town and London, 1870.

Castro, Fidel. *History Will Absolve Me*, London, 1968.

Chadhuri, N. C. *A Passage to England*, London, 1959.

Chalmers, J. A. *The Life of Tiyo Soga*, Edinburgh, 1877.

Clark, D. Stafford. *Psychiatry for Students*, 2nd edition, London, 1966.

Clark, Kenneth. *Civilization*, London, 1970.

Colson, E. *The Plateau Tonga*, Manchester, 1962.
Cox, Harvey. *The Secular City*, paperback edition, London, 1966.
Danquah, J. B. *The Akan Doctrine of God*, London, 1944, 2nd edition, 1968.
De Beauvoir, Simone, *A Very Easy Death*, Penguin edition, Harmondsworth, 1969.
De Chardin, Teilhard, *The Phenomenon of Man*, London, 1959.
De Jouvenel, B. *Sovereignty*, Cambridge, 1957.
De Vries, E. (ed.) *Man in Community*, New York, 1966.
Dieterlin, G. *Les Âmes des Dogons*, Paris, 1941.
Doke, C. M. and Vilakazi, B. W. *Zulu-English Dictionary*, Johannesburg, 1964.
Dollard, J. *Caste and Class in a Southern Town*, New York, 1937.
Douglas, Mary. *Purity and Danger*, London, 1966.
Eliot, T. S. *The Idea of a Christian Society*, London, 1939.
Epstein, A. L. *Politics in an Urban African Community*, Manchester, 1958.
Erikson, E. *Insight and Responsibility*, New York, 1964.
Evans-Pritchard, E. E. *Witchcraft, Oracles and Magic among the Azande*, Oxford, 1937.
Nuer Religion, Oxford, 1956.
Theories of Primitive Religion, Oxford, 1965.
Field, M. J. *Search for Security*, London, 1960.
Firth, Raymond, *Primitive Polynesian Economy*, London, 1939.
Forde, D. (ed.). *African Worlds*, London, 1954.
Forster, E. M. *Aspects of the Novel*, London, 1927.
Geertz, C. 'Religion as a Cultural System' in *Anthropological Approaches to the Study of Religion*, edited M. Banton, London, 1966.

Gluckman, M. (ed.). *Closed Systems and Open Minds*, Edinburgh, 1964.

Gorer, G. *Death, Grief and Mourning*, London, 1965.

Grahame, Kenneth. *The Wind in the Willows*, London, 1908.

Griaule, M. *Masques Dogons*, Paris, 1938.

Hancock, W. K. *Country and Calling*, London, 1954.

Hardy, Thomas. *The Mayor of Casterbridge*, London, 1895.

Hayward, V. E. W. (ed.). *African Independent Church Movements*, London, 1963.

Homans, G. C. *The Human Group*, London, 1951.

Hunter, Monica. *Reaction to Conquest*, London, 1936.

Huxley, Aldous. *Beyond the Mexique Bay*, 1934, Penguin edition 1955.

Huxley, Francis. *Affable Savages*, London, n.d.

Jabavu, D. D. T. *An African Independent Church*, Lovedale, 1942.

James, William. *The Varieties of Religious Experience*, London, 1902.

Junod, H. A. *The Life of a South African Tribe*, London, 1927, 2 vols.

Kaunda, K. *A Humanist in Africa*, London, 1966.

Krige, E. J. and J. D. *The Realm of a Rain Queen*, London, 1943.

Kropf, A. *A Kaffir-English Dictionary*, Lovedale, 1899.

Krüger, B. *The Pear Tree Blossoms*, Genadendal, 1968.

Kuper, H. *An African Aristocracy*, London, 1947.

Langer, Susanne. *Philosophy in a New Key*, Cambridge, Mass., 1942.

Laslett, Peter. *The World We have Lost*, London, 1965.

Leach, E. R. *A Runaway World?*, The Reith Lectures, 1967, London, 1968.

(ed.). *Dialectic in Practical Religion*, Cambridge, 1968.

Lewis, C. S. *The Allegory of Love*, Oxford, 1936.

Lienhardt, G. *Divinity and Experience*, Oxford, 1961.
Lorentz, K. *On Aggression*, London edition, 1966.
Macbeath, A. *Experiments in Living*, London, 1952.
Macmurray, John. *The Clue to History*, London, 1938.
The Boundaries of Science, London, 1939.
Maine, Henry. *Ancient Law*, London, 1876.
Marett, R. R. *The Threshold of Religion*, London, 2nd edition 1911.
Martin, M-L. *The Biblical Concept of Messianism and Messianism in the New Testament*, Morija, 1964.
Marwick, M. G. *Sorcery in its Social Setting*, Manchester, 1965.
Matthews, Z. K. (ed.). *Responsible Government in a Revolutionary Age*, New York, 1966.
Mead, M. *The American Character*, Pelican edition, 1944, first published in America as: ... *And Keep Your Powder Dry*, 1942.
Middleton, J. *Lugbara Religion*, London, 1960.
Moffat, Robert. *Missionary Labours and Scenes in Southern Africa*, London, 1842.
Moodie, D. *The Record*, 1838-42, reprint Cape Town, 1960; five parts.
Moore Smith, G. C. *The Letters of Dorothy Osborne to William Temple*, Oxford, 1928.
Mphahlele, E. *Down Second Avenue*, London, 1959.
Myrdal, G. *An American Dilemma*, New York, 1944.
Needham, J. *Time and Eastern Man*, Royal Anthropological Institute, London, 1965.
Newbigin, L. *Honest Religion for Secular Man*, London, 1966.
Niebuhr, H. Richard. *The Social Sources of Denominationalism*, 1929, paperback, Cleveland, 1957.
O'Brien, Connor Cruise. *The United Nations: Sacred Drama*, Hutchinson, 1968.

Oliver, R. *The Missionary Factor in East Africa*, London, 1952.

Oosthuizen, C. G. *Post Christianity in Africa*, London, 1968.

Otto, R. *The Idea of the Holy*, English translation, J. W. Harvey, London, 1926.

Pasternak, B. *Doctor Zhivago*, English translation, M. Hayward and M. Harari, London, 1958.

Pauw, B. A. *Religion in a Tswana Chiefdom*, Cape Town, 1960.

Radcliffe-Brown, A. R. *Structure and Function in Primitive Society*, London, 1952.

Ramsey, A. M. *Sacred and Secular*, London, 1965.

Redfield, Robert. *The Little Community*, Chicago, 1955.

The Folk Culture of Yucatan, Chicago, 1941.

A Village that Chose Progress, Chicago, 1950.

Richards, A. I. *Land, Labour and Diet in Northern Rhodesia*, London, 1939.

Chisungu, London, 1956.

Russell, C. and Russell, W. M. S. *Violence, Monkeys and Man*, London, 1968.

Russell, Bertrand. *The Impact of Science on Society*, London, 1952.

St Augustine. *The City of God*, translated by John Healey, London, 1931.

Silberbauer, G. B. *Bushman Survey*, Gaberones, 1965.

Smith, Adam. *The Wealth of Nations*, 1776; 1904 edition, London.

Smith, G. Adam. *The Book of Isaiah*, London, 1896, 2 vols.

Smuts, J. C. *Holism and Evolution*, London, 1926.

Sundkler, B. *Bantu Prophets in South Africa*, London, 1948.

Taylor, J. V. *The Primal Vision*, London, 1963.

Taylor, J. V. and Lehmann, D. *Christians of the Copperbelt*, London, 1961.

Temple, William. *Readings in St John's Gospel*, London, 1940.
Thomas, E. *The Harmless People*, London, 1959.
Thompson, E. P. *The Making of the English Working Class*, London, 1963.
Tillich, P. *Love, Power and Justice*, New York, 1960.
Toynbee, Arnold *et al. Man's Concern with Death*, London, 1968.
Turnbull, C. M. *The Forest People*, London, 1961.
Wayward Servants, London, 1966.
Turner, V. W. *The Forest of Symbols*, Ithaca, 1967.
The Drums of Affliction, Oxford, 1968.
The Ritual Process, Chicago, 1969.
Tylor, E. *Primitive Culture*, London, 1871.
Vidler, A. R. (ed.) *Soundings*, Cambridge, 1962.
Wach, Joachim. *The Sociology of Religion*, Chicago, 1944.
Ward, Barbara. *The Rich Nations and the Poor Nations*, London, 1962.
Warren, Max. *The Missionary Movement from Britain in Modern History*, London, 1965.
Waugh, E. *The Loved One*, London, 1948.
Weber, Max. *The Protestant Ethic and the Spirit of Capitalism*, paperback London, 1967.
Welbourn, F. B. *East African Rebels*, London, 1961.
Whitehead, A. N. *Adventures of Ideas*, Cambridge, 1933, paperback 1961.
Science in the Modern World, Pelican edition, 1938.
Williams, D. *When Races Meet*, Johannesburg, 1967.
Wilson, G. and M. *The Analysis of Social Change*, Cambridge, 1945.
Wilson, Monica. *Good Company*, London, 1951.
Rituals of Kinship among the Nyakyusa, London, 1957.
Communal Rituals of the Nyakyusa, London, 1959.

Wilson, M. and Mafeje, A. *Langa*, Cape Town, 1963.
Wilson, M. and Thompson, L. (eds). *The Oxford History of South Africa*, I, Oxford, 1969, II, 1970.
Wilson, M., Kaplan, S., Maki, T., Walton, E. M. *Social Structure*, Keiskammahoek Rural Survey, vol. III, Pietermaritzburg, 1952.
Wolfgang, M. E. and Ferracuti, F. *The Sub-Culture of Violence*, London, 1967.

ARTICLES AND REPORTS

Ali, Tariq. 'Gods and Guerrillas', *Punch*, 13 November 1968.
Beidelman, T. O. 'Three Tales of the Living and the Dead', *Journal of the Royal Anthropological Institute*, **94,** 2, 1964, 109-37.
'Right and Left Hand among the Kaguru', *Africa* **31,** 3, 1961, 250-7.
'Pig (Guluwe): An essay on Ngulu Sexual Symbolism and Ceremony', *Southwestern Journal of Anthropology*, **20**, 4, 1964, 359-92.
Bellah, R. N. 'Religious Evolution', *American Sociological Review*, **29,** 1964, 358-86.
'Civil Religion in America', *Daedalus*, **96,** 1, 1967, 1-21.
Berglund, A.-I. *Rituals of an African Bantu Church*, University of the Witwatersrand, Occasional Papers, 3.
'Fasting and Cleansing Rites' in *Concept of Death and Funeral Rites*, Report on the Missiological Institute, Umpumulo, Natal, 1968.
Boulding, K. E. 'Economics as a Moral Science', *American Economic Review*, **60,** 1, 1969, 1-12.
Crosse-Upcott, A. R. W. 'The Social Structure of the Ki-Ngindo-speaking Peoples', unpublished Ph.D. thesis, University of Cape Town, 1955.

Duthrie, G. I. 'Introduction', *King Lear*, New Shakespeare, Cambridge, 1960, xxxvi-xxxviii.

Fortes, Meyer. 'Ritual Festivals and Social Cohesion in the Hinterland of the Gold Coast', *American Anthropologist*, **38,** 4, 1936, 590-604.

Fortes, Doris and Meyer. 'Psychosis and Social Change Among the Tallensi of Northern Ghana', *Cahiers d'Etudes Africaines*, **21,** VI, 1966.

Gluckman, M. 'The Utility of the Equilibrium Model in the Study of Social Change', *American Anthropologist*, **70,** 2, 1968, 219-37.

Hammond-Tooke, W. D. 'Urbanization and the Interpretation of Misfortune', *Africa*, **40,** 1, 1970, 25-38.

Harlow, H. F. and Harlow, M. K. 'Social Deprivation in Monkeys', *Scientific American*, **207,** November 1962, 136-46.

Haselbarth, Hans. 'Why Seek Ye the Living among the Dead?', *Ministry*, Morija, July 1966.

Horrell, M. *A Survey of Race Relations in South Africa*, 1966, Johannesburg, 1967.

Hunter, Monica. 'An African Christian Morality', *Africa*, **10,** 1937, 265-91.

Ingram-Smith, T. 'The Trouble Behind the Trouble', *The Listener*, January 1967.

Jones, G. I. *Basutoland Medicine Murder*, H.M.S.O. 1951, Comd. 8209.

Leach, E. R. 'Magical Hair', *Journal of the Royal Anthropological Institute*, **88,** 11, 1958, 161.

'A Discussion on Ritualization of Behaviour in Animals and Man', *Philosophical Transactions of the Royal Society*, London, 1966, B.772, vol. 251.

Licko, Pavel. 'A Visit to Solzhenitzyn', *The Listener*, 20 March 1969.

MacQuarrie, J. W. *The Main Needs for the Future in African Education*, South African Institute of Race Relations Conference, Johannesburg, 1969.

Marwick, M. G. 'Another Modern Anti-Witchcraft Movement in East Central Africa', *Africa*, **20,** 1950, 100-12.

Mason, P. 'Human Rights and Race Relations', unpublished lecture.

Naudé, The Rev. Beyers. *Pro Veritate*, 1968.

Paton, A. 'A Personal View', *British Medical Journal*, 6 September 1969.

Raine, Kathleen. 'A Traditional Language of Symbols', *The Listener*, 9 October 1958.

Richards, A. I. 'A Modern Movement of Witchfinders', *Africa*, **8,** 1935, 448-61.

'Social Mechanisms for the Transfer of Political Rights in Some African Tribes', *Journal of the Royal Anthropological Institute*, **90,** 2, 1960, 175-90.

'Keeping the King Divine', *Proceedings of the Royal Anthropological Institute* for 1968, London, 1969, 23-35.

Rigby, P. 'Dual Symbolic Classification among the Gogo of Central Tanzania', *Africa*, **36,** 1, 1966, 1-17.

'Some Gogo Rituals of Purification', *Dialectic in Practical Religion*, edited E. R. Leach, Cambridge, 1968.

'The Structural Context of Girls' Puberty Rites', *Man*, **2,** 3, 1967, 434-44.

Serpell, C. 'Golden Bough over the East River', *The Listener*, 30 May 1968.

Setiloane, G. 'Frontier Meditation', *Frontier*, February 1969, pp. 19-22.

Sonnabend, H. 'Demographic Samples in the Study of Backward and Primitive Populations', *South African Journal of Economics*, **2,** 1934, 319-21.

Stewart, J. *African Papers*, No. 1 n.d.

T'Hooft, Visser. 'Modernizing without Compromising', *The Listener*, 9 March 1967, p. 327.

Ward, Barbara. *A New History*, Davie Memorial Lecture, University of Cape Town, 1969.

Williams, H. A. *The Suffering of Mankind*, address in Coventry Cathedral, December 1966.

Wilson, Godfrey. 'An African Morality', *Africa* **9**, 1936, 75-98.

'Anthropology as a Public Service', *Africa*, **13**, 1940, 45-59.

Wilson, Monica, 'Witch Beliefs and Social Structure', *American Journal of Sociology*, **56**, 4, 1951, 307-13.

Report . . . of the Government Commission on Native Laws and Customs, Cape Town, 1883, G.4-'83.

Report of the Native Churches Commission, U.G. 39, '25.

Report of Native Affairs Commission on the Israelites, A.4-21.

INDEX